Speakers' Corner Anthology

Jim Huggon, editor

Union of Egoists
Baltimore 2022

Speakers' Corner Anthology by Jim Huggon
Copyright © 2022 Jim Huggon
Foreword © 2022 Estate of Philip Sansom
All rights reserved.

Cover Design by Kevin I. Slaughter
Interior Design by Trevor Blake

London: Kropotkin's Lighthouse Publications 1977
Baltimore: Union of Egoists 2022

Special thanks from the Union of Egoists to Fred Woodworth. Read *The Match!* Post Office Box 3012, Tucson Arizona 85702 United States.

Stand Alone SA1227

Huggon, Jim
[English]
Speakers' Corner Anthology
ISBN 978-1-944651-26-8
1. London
2. Free Speech
Jim Huggon

The Union of Egoists publishes rare work and original research related to Max Stirner and the philosophy of egoism circa 1845-1945.

UnionOfEgoists.com

127 House: At every turn in its thought society will find us waiting.

Contents

Foreword .... Philip Sansom 5
Acknowledgements .... Jim Huggon 13
New Edition .... Jim Huggon 15
Tyburn .... Jim Huggon 19
Speakers' Corner .... Jim Huggon 21
An Encyclopedia of London (excerpt) .... William Kent 23
Against the Sunday Trading Bill .... Karl Marx 27
The Hyde Park Railway to Reform .... Royden Harrison 37
Tom Mann and His Times (excerpt) .... Dona Torr 43
The First London May Day (excerpt) .... Star 49
Militant Suffragettes (excerpt) .... Antonia Raeburn 51
Christian Evidence .... Guy Aldred 57
"Personalities and Places" .... Bonar Thompson 65
The Black Hat .... Bonar Thompson 71
Freedom in the Park .... George Orwell 85
Freedom Defence Committee Bulletin (excerpt) 89
Tower Hill 12.30 (excerpt) .... Donald Soper 91
"On the Platform" .... Horatio 103
Stop Speaking, I'm Interrupting! .... Dusty Hughes 107
"Triumph of Stage Irishman" .... Guardian 115
Park Regulations 117
Bibliography .... Jim Huggon 125

Further Reading .... Union of Egoists 131

Illustrations

Front and Back Covers, First Edition 13
"To Axel... " 14
Guy Aldred 57, 62
Emma Goldman 55
Jim Huggon 17
Tom Mann 47
S. E. Parker 100
John Rety 22
Philip Sansom 5
Donald Soper 101
The Speakers 114
Ben Tillett 35
Bonar Thompson 26, 84, 147
Jacobus Van Dyn 129

Foreword

Philip Sansom

COMRADES and Friends!
We owe a considerable debt of gratitude to Jim Huggon for the work he has put into this collection of documents on Hyde Park, for he has gathered a great deal of background information on that unique place.

My qualifications for contributing are purely personal. I spoke from the platform of the London Anarchist Group at Hyde Park practically every Sunday from 1947 to 1960, come rain or shine, and gave little thought to the struggles that a made possible my exercise of "free" speech.

What is a little sobering today is to reflect that over those thirteen years I must have spoken well over five hundred times, uttering millions of words to thousands of people with, as far as I can see, precious little effect in terms of influencing events.

Even to say that now seems ridiculous, for who in their right mind would consider Hyde Park if they were setting out to influence events? Perhaps a massive rally might end up there, made complete with public address system — but even that would be aimed at influencing the passage of a Bill through Parliament rather than events themselves.

The struggles described in the documents gathered by our our Editor — himself a consistent Hyde Park Speaker with an amiable and conversational manner just as persuasive in its way as the more oratorical and rabble-rousing manner that I adopted — shows beyond doubt that when the Park was first seized by the people as a public forum it was seen as a centre from which the "will of the masses" could radiate.

But our ruling class knows a thing or two worth a dozen of that; it knows where the real power lies, how to defuse "public opinion" (whatever that is), how to manipulate it and how advantageous it is in a "democracy" to have a unique institution like Speakers' Corner all neatly railed in and so supervised by the police.

Even before the emergence of our modern mass media, the main political parties had little use for Hyde Park. The first four years of my speaking career' — 1947-1951 — were spent under the immediate post-war Government of Clement Attlee, during which major nationalisation Bills went through Parliament, India was granted independence, Britain commenced production of atomic weapons, conscription was continued, bread was rationed and lots of "important" things were done in our name.

But I cannot remember a single occasion when a Labour Party platform appeared in Hyde Park with even minor party hacks speaking to the people of London face-to-face, let alone Cabinet Ministers. They spoke to the people over the radio, and even when they did appear in public, at, say, official May Day rallies they spoke through loud speakers, with no more danger of actual dialogue with "the masses" than when on the BBC.

This is not to say, however, that no notice is ever taken by the authorities of activities at Hyde Park. Obviously, if a demonstration gathers large enough support it must be indicative of some measure of feeling in the community at large. Those who go to the trouble of marching and supporting rallies are always only a small proportion of those agreeing with its aims, whatever they are. Notice is taken of a rally strictly, one imagines, in proportion to the numbers taking part and the importance to the government of the day of the issue being protested.

Thus, thirty thousand women demonstrating on abortion will carry more weight with a government than one hundred and fifty thousand men, women and children demanding the abolition of the nuclear bomb, for the carefully controlled legalisation of abortion is something the government will yield on — but it will not give up its weapons of terror.

All that the massive demonstrations of the Sixties against The Bomb can be said to have achieved was to push the government to agree to halt in the above-ground testing of H-bombs. Big deal! I am cynical enough to believe that the states signing that agreement had already got as much information as they needed at that time and were quite prepared to stop testing in the air (while continuing underground!) and it was quite a useful exercise in public relations to allow it to be thought that "concerned public opinion" (as represented on the CND marches by MPs like Michael Foot) had been taken into account in, not banning the bomb, but by banning the testing of the bomb in the atmosphere.

Yet public relations is what Hyde Park is all about. For its real importance is not as a place from which the people tell it what to do, but as a meeting place for the people to talk to each other. And for this purpose the face-to-face dialogue is essential, providing as it does the possibility of answering back.

And why shouldn't the people be allowed to talk to each other? Faced with the immense power of the media - more insidious in its hidden forms, with ingrown assumptions and potted "expert" opinions, than in the overt Party Political Broadcasts which we all turn off anyway, the face-to-face public meeting, whether indoors or out, remains the only true means available for the immediate and spontaneous exchange of ideas.

Those of us who have been asked to take part in any programme on the TV know that although it is self-defeating to refuse to take part, it is also most frustrating to appear, the programme controllers have you firmly in their grip and unless you are the "star" — and none of *us* ever is — you are lucky to get two breathless minutes in which to give your tuppence-worth of solutions to the world's problems. That's if the programme goes out live. If it is filmed and goes out later, edited, you may be cut out altogether — certainly what you thought of as your best bits always are!

But on the platform at Hyde Park, that's a different matter. Once you have mastered the ability either to ignore, out-shout or competently deal with interruptions, then you are the master of the situation. It's a live performance, folks, and you stand or fall by what you say — most of which is unprepared and off the top of your head. Which gives it all a certain magic and uncertainty, for nobody can talk for the sort of time that the experienced Hyde Park speaker would consider normal (from one to six or eight hours every Sunday something which would slay your average politician) and do it over the years, without from time to time making a fool of yourself. That's something you have to be prepared to do.

I am not going to recount here the one or two incidents which still make me blush to think of, nor recall the dull gatherings when I stumbled and mumbled and bored myself because I had no inspiration and was dying for a heckler to come to my aid, nor the cold and empty park in winter, talking only to the faithful converted.

No, I prefer to remember the good times: long hot summer afternoons with tightly packed and silent crowds of maybe three or four hundred, spellbound when I was really on form, or the lively, swaying meetings when the audience would be falling about with laughter one minute and the next holding back their tears as I switched to the horror of, say, the Sharpeville massacre, or whatever war was going on at the time. Anger and laughter, love and hate, idealism and bitterness — all play their part in revolutionary oratory.

Oddly enough, the two most successful meetings which stay in my memory were not at Hyde Park. The first was at Denison House, in Victoria in March 1953, when I debated on behalf of the London Anarchist Group with Tony Turner of the Socialist Party of Great Britain. Tony was a great speaker, best of a very good and capable bunch of speakers that the SPGB had at that time, and it is on record that he spoke at the Park for ten hours non-stop on the day war was declared in 1939. The LAG and the SPGB had an unspoken pact in the Park: we didn't heckle their meetings and they didn't heckle ours. This not due to any friendliness between the two organisations, but simply that we each knew that the speaker has the advantage, and can usually make the heckler look silly.

But the SPGB were very fond of organising debates and the time came when I got the invitation to debate with the man (though nobody in the party would have admitted *that*!). I had taken the precaution of going to SPGB meetings and debates and learned how they went to work — and I went to work in exactly the same way. Unlike unsuspecting Liberals or Labourites I knew what they were going to say, and I set out to spike their guns by saying it first and fortunately the rules of the debate, as they played them, worked in my favour.

I had the opening word and the closing summing-up, with Tony sandwiched in between. He was never able to get the initiative and the superiority of the anarchist case, when expounded in the fundamentalist way which is usually the SPGB's greatest weapon, won the day, to the consternation of the party members.

The SPGB has never been quite the same since and I was amused to note that in the annals of successful debates in which their opponents were slaughtered, they don't even mention Denison House, 1st March 1953!

The second of my fondest memories dates from 1956, when the LAG held its usual meeting at Manette Street in Charing Cross Road at the height of the Suez/Hungary invasions.

While both equally tragic and bloody, the coincidence of these two imperialist adventures was a gift to the anarchists. So often, on our platform, we attack the British or the Americans, to be denounced as

Communists, or we attack the communists, to be denounced as agents of Western Imperialism — and that is putting it politely.

The last gasp of Britain's gun-boat imperialism and the first blast of Russia's land-locked imitation of the same, with tanks entering Budapest, coincided in the last week of October 1956. We had been holding meetings at Manette Street (that's the little street between the two Foyle's bookshops in Charing Cross Road) for about two years previously and had built up a ready audience. On the evening of Saturday, 27th October, the crowd was already waiting when we arrived.

In no time at all it was much bigger than usual. Feeling was running high in the country about Eden's invasion of Egypt and the added tragedy of what was happening in Hungary aggravated public interest in any meeting that was going on. Very soon, policeman arrived and we were ordered to stop the meeting. I got off our small platform and spoke to the constable (his very presence attracted more people) and then told him that I would get back on the stand to tell the crowd that we were having to stop.

This I did (with tongue in cheek) and went on to tell the unusually large crowd that we had held meetings here without interference for two years and here was an attempt to take away our — and *their* — freedom of speech. By the time I had finished my "closing" remarks the crowd was incensed and began to roar "Carry on — we're with you!" and similar words of support.

So what could I do, constable? We had to carry on. By the time an Inspector and two more PCs arrived the crowd was much too big to be dispersed by the police peacefully. I was really steaming full ahead on the anti-war issue, the Communist perfidy in Budapest, the disgusting nature of government in general and the traffic was being blocked right across Charing Cross Road. We went on for two hours with a perfectly orderly public meeting, whipped up an enormous amount of support, sold a record number of *Freedoms* and closed tired and happy in time for a pint at the Hercules in Greek Street.

Great days! And if I have spoken only of my own activities as a speaker I must here mention others in our group without whom we could not have done as much as we did.

My own companion for nine years, Rita Milton, developed quickly into an effective speaker. Her sharp and aggressive tongue and her jutting chin made up for her diminutive stature and made her more than a match for any heckler. Women Speakers were - and still are — rare in Hyde Park, where a strong voice is such an asset, but Rita had her own following, particularly as she chose to concentrate very much on the misdeeds and sexual repressiveness of the Catholic Church — and indeed the Christians in general.

We encouraged other speakers: John Bishop, black mustachioed in the Zapata style before it became popular, with a good voice and delivery who worked hard at putting over the anarchist case. He was full of humour in private conversation but somehow, unhappily, could not put it across on the platform. Frank Hirshfield, who can let it hang out anywhere, was a natural, using cheeky Jewish phrases and a rather surrealist approach with which he could always confuse the opposition if not convince them. Donald Rooum, with an enormously loud Yorkshire voice when he chose to open up, which he occasionally did with devastating logic and effect, though normally he had a friendly and conversational approach enriched with wry humour. Jack Rubin, one of a brilliant bunch of South African Jews who came to Britain when the Nationalists gained power in 1948. The shy Jim Peeke, who spoke with surprising confidence once we pushed him up on the platform; even, for a time, before overwhelmed with individualism, Sid Parker.

That group was followed in the Sixties by John Rety, practically the last of the "group" speakers. John was an amusing speaker with whom the crowd felt it easy to relate.

This is an important factor and one which the serious Marxists and Christians have not managed to integrate into their historical messages. They don't realise the importance of sugaring the pill of propaganda with sweet entertainment. Another more than useful speaker on the the platform at this time was John Pilgrim.

An off-shoot of the anarchists, if he will forgive me describing him, was Axel Ney-Hoch, anarchistic all right, but too individualist to ever be a kosher member of our group. An habitue of the anarchist's Malatesta Club, Axel was endearing and infuriating by turns — characteristics which, of course, make for a great Hyde Park speaker.

He is one of the four speakers featured in "The Speakers"[1], and I would like to thank him here for some nice words he said about me when being interviewed on *Radio London* just before the recent revival of that play by Heathcote Williams at the Conway Hall. A wierd production. I did not know the other three speakers portrayed and of the portrait of Axel I can only say that the artistic reproduction did not come up to the original. But then, what does?

I had begun speaking in 1947 through the encouragement of our old comrade Mat Kavanagh, an Irish anarchist whose militancy dated back to World War I. I paced the ground at Speakers' Corner many Sundays before finally screwing up my courage and asking to be allowed up on to the platform. All the fine phrases I had worked out in advance were used up in the first five minutes — and then, to my surprise, were followed by others I had not thought of before. I stayed up for over half an hour (chiefly because the other comrades had all walked off for a cup of tea and left me there!), and then, for over five hundred Sundays afterwards, they just couldn't keep me off the platform. To say nothing of those

---

[1] See Bibliography. The play is Heathcote Williams' own adaption of his book.

Saturdays at Manette Street and Tuesdays at Tower Hill! Oratory can become a drug, there's no doubt about that. You can, in the funny old phrase, become inebriated with the exuberance of your own verbosity. The extent to which you get enmeshed in the activity, though, depends upon whether, like the "professionals," you are dependent upon speaking for a living, and also upon the satisfactions you gain from other activities in your life.

Fortunately, though I have enjoyed many stimulants, I have taken care never to become dependent upon any one. I was able to stand outside of myself as an experienced speaker and see the dangers of what I could do. After quite unconsciously learning various techniques I slowly became aware that I could manipulate a crowd as surely as a shepherd manipulates his dog. I realised that I had learned how to lift them up and put down, stir them this way or that.

The essence of my message had always been to encourage individualist to think for themselves, not to think like me, and the danger of being persuasive is that they were simply replacing one source of opinion with another instead of making up their own minds. It was a dangerous skill I had acquired and from an anarchist point of view, not what I had set out to do. I decided to give it all a rest.

Nevertheless, I am as prone to flattery as most, and still get gratification out of bumping into people who remember those Sunday afternoons with as much pleasure as I do. Having to rush for a train at Kings Cross recently I hailed a taxi. As I settled into the back seat the driver slid back the glass panel and said "The last time I saw you must have been about fifteen years ago - speaking at the Park." We, of course, rapped away until we reached the station and then, as I reached for my change, he said "No, have this one on me."

In spite of my (feeble) protests he put up his flag and as he drove off, called out "Stick to yer principles!" Which made my day.

So what of my anarchist principles? Well, they haven't changed, even if I don't parade them in public so much now. But then neither has the world changed, in any fundamental, social, sense. What has happened is that in many personal ways — the ways which anarchists regard as of prime importance, many changes have taken place.

The capitalists may still hold property deeds which say they own the world — but thousands of squatters in houses and hundreds of workers occupying factories prove with their presence that there is something else to be taken into consideration. The churches may still thunder their moralities but millions of free-thinking men and women live and love without benefit of clergy. States may still rattle their sabres, but after Vietnam the most powerful state on earth knows that its young men will never again be meekly minced into canon fodder.

They are individuals who squat and occupy; individuals who fuck without guilt and who desert from the army with honour among their peers.

They are individuals that you speak to at Hyde Park. Although in a crowd emotions can be swayed in ways distinct from personal conversation, still it is that face-to-face situation that matters. You are not just a talking head on a goggle-box and you can be answered back — and while the speaker on a platform always has an advantage, he can still be made to listen, still, in extreme cases, get a punch on the nose. It is the spread of ideas on the human scale — and I maintain that the anarchist social revolution must be preceded by millions of personal revolutions, so that "the fabric of our society" is in shreds before we have to put anything in its place.

Well... perhaps some of those millions of words to thousands of people on hundreds of Sunday afternoons have borne fruit after all. If one in a thousand was encouraged to find the strength to disobey, we have done something.

Quite apart from any possibility of social consequences, though, I have to say that the experience on the platform was good for *me*. For developing self-confidence; for building a healthy ego in a healthy body (think of all those lungs-full of fresh air blasted out in the summer sunshine!), there's nothing quite like speaking in Hyde Park. And what's more, you are forced to find out what you really think.

As dear old Bonar Thompson, one of the greatest of them all once said to me: "I have learnt all I know by listening to myself speak!"

Acknowledgements

by Jim Huggon

FIRSTLY my thanks are due to all the authors, editors and publishers whose material is contained in this anthology. I've fully acknowledged the source of each written extract or illustration where it appears, except for the item by Karl Marx ("agitation against the Sunday Trading Bill") which was reprinted from *Karl Marx: Surveys from Exile*, edited by David Fenbach and published by Penguin and New Left Review (1973), and Bonar Thompson's book *Hyde Park Orator*, which was published by Jarrolds in 1934. Special thanks are also due to Lord Soper for permission to reprint the extract from his book *Tower Hill 12.30* (Epworth Press).

The Front Cover photograph of Ben Tillett was reproduced from *Banner Bright* by John Gorman (published by Allen Lane 1973). I am also deeply indebted to many others; to Stephanie Cloete, Jo Foster and Lynn Alderson who typed their way stoically through my illegible scrawl.

To Sue Mister and Julia Thomas who duplicated the stencils.

To Arthur Moyse who drew the beautiful covers. To Philip Sansom for writing the foreword, and for permission to reproduce the photos that accompany it.

To Sharley and Jeannie McLean who first introduced me to Speakers' Corner many years ago, and thus to countless hours of listening and speaking pleasure. To John Rety who gave me my first chance to "have a go" on the anarchist platform, and thus to acquire a taste — if not a skill — that I have never lost. To Philip Sansom — again — and Robert Ogilvie — the two finest speakers I ever heard in Hyde Park.

To Peter Turner for unearthing the copy of Bonar Thompson's *Black Hat* reproduced herein.

To the police of Hyde Park not only for their help in the preparation of this book, but also for their good natured tolerance every weekend which allows us, the speakers - for the most part — to bend, if not break, the regulations.

To all my immediate predecessors and contemporaries on the anarchist platform in Hyde Park — in addition to Philip and John, from all of whom I learned a great deal - Desmond MacDonald, John Pilgrim, Nigel Wilson and Bill Dwyer.

To all the speakers, listeners, hecklers, tourists of Hyde Park, without whom... To all of them, my warmest thanks.

A Short Note on the Extracts

I think most of the extracts, their sources and their reasons for inclusion are self-explanatory. My "editorial policy" — such as it is — being to include virtually whatever I could find that was relevant; but I should say that I have included the Hyde Park Regulations and the various Statutory Instruments associated with them, in full in an endeavour to show — as if it were necessary — that Hyde Park's much vaunted "Freedom of Speech" is, in reality, a myth.

"To Axel / my old friend / with much love. / Jim Huggon"

New Edition

by Jim Huggon

I spoke on the "Hyde Park anarchist" Platform for eighteen years — from 1965 to 1983. At one time, briefly, we had *three* anarchist platforms at Speakers' Corner because our views on anarchism were so different (which is — of course — as it should be).

I am also a violinist. I spent twenty years (1984 - 2004) earning my living playing on the streets. I also played — though not for money — in orchestras, string orchestras, string quartets and the opera houses in London. But that is all another story!

In 1977 I edited and published *Speakers' Corner, An Illustrated Anthology*, of writings by speakers and about speakers plus photos and illustrations, until now out of print and quite rare. It included substantial extracts from Bonar Thompsons' autobiography plus a photo of Bonar in his famous black hat, plus a reproduction in full of his famous but now very rare journal *The Black Hat*.

I never saw or heard Thompson speak. I came to Speakers' Corner around 1965. So I arrived on the scene too late for Thompson.

I met Donald Rooum in the early Sixties, when I had just left school. We were both members of the militant anti-war group The Committee of One Hundred. I knew Leslie Jenson in the 1970s and '80s but I am pretty sure he is dead now.

You may reprint my book on Speakers' Corner. One or two suggestions on that. I would suggest re-ordering one or two items. Specifically, putting the Hyde Park Regulations at the back of the book as a sort of appendix, not in the front. I think they are important in that some people still think that freedom of speech in the speaking area is absolute. Far from it! Although I was only thrown out of the park once in eighteen years, it was only because I obeyed the *unwritten* rules operating in the park. Others were thrown out more often. In practice you *could* say what you liked. The cops did not like obscenity and if you insulted them directly — but *indirectly* you could get away with a great deal if you spoke with a little care and humour.

There is one item I discovered years later. It is contained in Rudolph Rocker's *The London Years* pp. 86-89. This book was very rare in the 1970s when I published my tome. A friend in Canada sent me a copy of the first edition years later. It was reprinted in 2005. I would have included the pages mentioned above.

In an otherwise favorable review the *Socialist Standard* (organ of the Socialist Party of Great Britain, by far the oldest Marxist party here) was critical of Philip Sanson's introduction to my book. But I would not pay too much attention to that. The late Philip Sanson was, in his day (roughly 1947 - 1963), one of the very finest Hyde Park speakers on the anarchist platform.

The Speakers by Heathcote Williams had quite a vogue in its day but I am a little critical of it. The few speakers it treats specifically are MacGuinness, Webster, Jacobus Van Dyn and Axel Ney Hoch. MacGinness I never knew, but the other three I did. Van Dyn was tattooed from head to foot — allegedly because he was once nicked in a case of mistaken identity and so went out and got himself tattooed all over so that no one would ever mistake himself for anyone else ever again! In the 1970s I knew him because he was a sort of permanent model in a tattoo parlour in Kings Cross, North London, around the corner from Housmans Bookshop where I used it as a sort of business address in addition to working for the bookshop for thirteen years (1969 - 1982). Housmans is still there. It is owned by Peace News. It still sells radical literature!

Tragically at the end of his life Jacobus Van Dyn developed cancer of the throat and lost his voice. He used to flip through a considerable collection of photos of himself (as you can imagine) to anybody who would care to look, silently sitting in Hyde Park.

Webster was a fine speaker. He would spend our winter in the the Domain, in Sydney, Australia (ie their summer). When he could make enough money in the weekly collection (easier there than here) to return here for our summer (their winter). The Domain in Sydney was famous as Australia's Speakers' Corner. Still is, I think.

Axel Ney Hock has a chapter to himself. It is the book that I gave him that you have. Axel was a fine speaker with a fine voice. Axel lodged for a while with Alan and Sharley McLean. I went out with their daughter Jeanie for four years in the late 1960s. We ended up living together — disastrously — for six months. I was introduced to Speakers' Corner by Jeanie. Jeanie had been coming to Speakers' Corner since the age of minus nine months. Sharley (Jeanie's mother) many years later spoke herself at the corner on the gay and lesbian platform. Quite successfully too. There were — and are — far too few women speakers and even fewer good ones, sadly. I last met Sharley at her home in 2006. She and Alan are now dead as is Axel and all the others!

I hope all this is of interest.

Heigh Ho!

Jim Huggon

Tyburn

Jim Huggon

SPEAKERS' Corner stands on the spot once occupied by the infamous Tyburn Gallows, the custom of giving the intended victim "a few last words" to the crowd assembled to see his or her end being perpetuated in the soap box oratory of today. Other former places of public execution also gave rise eventually to similar traditional rights to speak in that place, but of these others only Tower Hill survives to my knowledge.

As a place of public execution Tyburn dates back to the Twelfth Century, although the original Tyburn may not have been at Marble Arch. However, among the worthies executed at Tyburn where it eventually stood at Marble Arch were Perkin Warbeck — pretender to the English throne (1499), the Holy Maid of Kent (1535), John Felton, the murderer of Villiers, the Duke of Buckingham (1628) and John (Jack) Sheppard, highwayman (1724).

In 1661, the skeletons of Cromwell, Ireton and others were hung for demonstration on the gallows, Cromwell having died of natural causes in 1658, and having been dug up especially for the occasion! The last execution at Tyburn took place in 1783, thereafter executions taking place at Newgate.

Although the use of Hyde Park as a venue for public meetings dates back to the early part of the Nineteenth Century, the *right* to legally speak there — subject of course to the many regulations "enforced" in the place — dates back only to 1872.

Happily however, Nelson is often to be found wearing a police uniform and often, though not always, self-restraint, tolerance good humour prevail, together with not a little tact and judgement on both "sides."

It should also be said that although the antics of the speakers may occasionally test the patience of the London Bobby to breaking point, the authorities generally can have no real intention of threatening the Park for it as well serves their purpose (as a safety valve, a tourist attraction and, regrettably, occasionally it seems almost a zoo!) as it serves ours as speakers, as a serious public forum for debate, discussion, entertainment and enlightenment.

Speakers' Corner

Jim Huggon

THE suitability of Hyde Park for meetings was first realised by a group of shopkeepers, who, in July 1855 applied to Sir Richard Mayne, the Commissioner of Police, for permission to hold a meeting there to protest about the Sunday Trading Bill. Mayne forbade this.

In October 1855, a carpenter collected an audience of curious passers-by, by speaking in the park and as he had not officially notified the police of his intentions, he was ignored by the authorities; in subsequent weeks he was joined by more militant speakers and then police were called in to quell riotous behaviour.

Police supervision of the park prevented further meetings until 1859 when an extremely large crowd gathered to demonstrate their support for the Emperor Napoleon in his invasion of Italy. In 1862 a similar meeting was held to pledge support for Garibaldi.

In 1866, Speakers' Corner as we think of it today began; the projected Reform Bill of that year was objected to by a large number of people. The Reform League was formed in opposition to the bill, and the leaders of the league applied to Mayne for permission to hold a meeting — he refused — and went so far as to make arrangements for the police to guard the park.

The League expressed its intention of going ahead anyway. As the leaders of the demonstration approached the park they saw that the gates had been shut and they were guarded by considerable numbers of both foot and mounted police. The leaders turned away but a considerable disturbance took place. The crowd uprooted railings and poured into the park to hold a meeting. During the meeting tree branches were torn off, one particular tree in the centre of the meeting was selected, and branches piled around it; this was set on fire reducing it to a charred stump. It became known as Reformers' Tree.

As the demonstration left behind two hundred and sixty injured policemen and a trail of wreckage in its wake, the next application to hold a meeting there was viewed with much trepidation by Mayne. In consultation with the Commissioner of Works, it was decided that the meeting would be held at an area now known as the meeting ground, this was about one hundred and fifty yards from Reformers' Tree.

In October 1872, legislation[1] was introduced to control meetings at Speakers' Corner, a notice board was erected at the meeting ground and all meetings had to be held within forty yards of it, persons wishing to speak were required to apply at the office of H. M. Ministry of works

---

[1] Sunday Trading Bill — see article by Karl Marx.

and Public Buildings at least two days in advance. Only one meeting was allowed at a time.

The situation today is rather different. Many different meetings go on at once, and many very large rallies have been held, mostly without incident. Probably the largest of these was at Easter 1963, when between 100,000 and 150,000 people attended the Easter Rally of the Campaign for Nuclear Disarmament.

John Rety

An Encyclopedia of London (excerpt)

William Kent

HYDE Park (360 acres) was in Saxon times the manor of Eis — from which later the name "Hyde" was derived. On a pedestal supporting a vase at the east end of the Serpentine is the following inscription: "A supply of water by conduit from this spot was granted to the Abbey of Westminster with the Manor of Hyde by King Edward the Confessor. The Manor was resumed by the Crown in 1736, but preserved to the Abbey by the Charter of Queen Elizabeth in 1560."

It appears first to have been enclosed by the Abbot and convent Westminster. In the reign of Henry VIII (1536) it passed into the possession of the Crown. By 1637 it had become a public park: it was then used for horse-racing. In 1652 the Commonwealth Government sold it into private hands, and Evelyn records that "every coach was made to pay a shilling, and a horse sixpence, by the sordid fellow who had purchased it." It must have seemed an avenging Nemesis that led to Cromwell's accident when he was driving a coach.

Carlyle wrote: "The horses, beautiful animals, tasting of the whip, became unruly; galloped would not be checked, but took to plunging; plunged the postillion down; plunged or shook his Highness down, dragging him by the foot for some time so that 'a pistol went off in his pocket' to the amazement of men. Whereupon? Whereupon — his Highness got up again, little the worse; was let blood; and went about his affairs much as usual!"

At the Restoration in 1660, the contract of sale was cancelled, and Hyde Park once more became a favorite *rendezvous* of fashion, as well as a convenient place for military reviews. It was then enclosed by a brick wall, which stood until 1726. In 1730 the *élite* played cricket in the Park, the players including the Dukes of Devonshire and Richmond and the Earl of Albemarle. In the same year the Serpentine lake was formed by order of Queen Caroline (consort of George II), from the flow of the river Westbourne (see *Lost Rivers*). In 1749 Horace Walpole was robbed in Hyde Park by the famous highwayman McLean. In 1768 — for the last time — there was Royal hunting there; Christian VII of Denmark joined his brother-in-law George III in hunting, but only a single buck was allowed to be shot. In 1769 the *Public Advertiser* informed its readers that General Paoli of Corsica "accompanied by James Boswell, Esq., took an airing in Hyde Park in his coach. His Excellency came out and took a walk by the Serpentine River and through Kensington Gardens with which he seemed very much pleased."

The elder Pitt, the Earl of Chatham, was the first to call the park "the lungs of London." It was a great place for duels. The most notable was between Lord Mohum and the Fourth Duke of Hamilton in 1712 when both combatants were killed. This encounter is immortalized in Thackeray's *Henry Esmond*. In the Eighteenth Century there were many robberies and a bell was rung at intervals to mobilize people who were about to cross it en route to town. In 1784 the Serpentine was frozen, and the Earl of Carlisle, Benjamin West and Dr. Hewitt danced minuets on the ice. In 1803 two respectable tradesmen aged 73 and 62 engaged in a race over a course of one hundred yards. In honour of a single cossack — Russia having, it was held, saved Europe from Napoleon — so many as one hundred thousand people are said to have assembled in the park in 1813. In 1814, for the first time since 1357 — when John of France was brought prisoner after the battle of Poitiers — a French King was in London. Louis XVIII went to Hyde Park attended by an imposing cavalcade, and was accompanied by the Prince Regent. In the same year, by way of a centenary celebration of the ascension of the House of Hanover to the British throne, a miniature battle of Trafalgar was staged on the Serpentine. In 1818 a band of Canadian Indians, each in war-dress and bearing a tomahawk, attracted a huge crowd. In 1825 the brick wall in Park Lane, and between Hyde Park Corner and Kensington, was taken down and replaced by iron railings. In the same year a son of Henry Hunt, a notorious radical, drove a four-in-hand over the frozen Serpentine.

In the Victorian era it became the greatest resort of popular orators. In July 1855 it was proposed to hold a huge open-air meeting there to protest against a Sunday Trading Bill. Sir Richard Mayne, Commissioner of Police, opposed it, and no meeting was held. On 14th October 1855 a carpenter addressed a meeting there, and, finding no interference, repeated the performance on the following Sunday. He then congratulated his audience on again exercising their own recognized privilege of meeting in "their own park." On 28th October, 4th, 11th, and 18th November, there were further meetings, riotous in character; on the last date there was a strong force of police in attendance to disperse the crowd. There were no further meetings until 1859. In that year one was held to present an address to the Emperor Napoleon, sympathizing with him in the course he had taken respecting Italy. In 1862, at meetings in support of Garibaldi, there was some blood shed. In 1866 a monster meeting was to be held in Hyde Park, organized by the Reform League. Sir Richard Mayne prohibited it. On being denied admission, the demonstrators tore down hundreds of yards of iron railings and swarmed into the park. The serious riot that followed led eventually to a more conciliatory attitude towards the right of meeting which was persistently claimed, and in 1872 the Commissioner of Works definitely assigned a certain spot one hundred and fifty yards from the "Reformer's Tree" — the place where meetings of the Reform League had been held — for such assemblies. From that time "Orator's Corner" has been one of London's attractions. Here "every splintered fraction of a sect" finds utterances; and G. K. Chesterton, wishing to indicate the sorrows of a really limited monarchy, pointed out that our sovereigns alone were not allowed to a little tub-thumping in Hyde Park. A fascinating book on this subject is *Hyde Park Orator* by Bonar Thompson (1934). For many years the author earned his living by exuberant and cynical verbosity, making an average of £2 10s per week in Summer n £1 15s in Winter, despite the fact that, owing to regulations, contributions can be received only outside the gates. He suggests as his epitaph: "The Collection Was Not Enough." Other books are *Around the Marble Arch* by F. W. Batchelor (1944) and *A Saint in Hyde Park* by E. A. Siderman (1950). The "saint" was Father Vincent McNabb of St. Dominic's Priory. This book has a well-merited popularity.

Bonar Thompson

Agitation Against the Sunday Trading Bill

Karl Marx

London, 25th June

OBSOLETE social forces, nominally still in possession of all the attributes of power long after the basis of their existence has rotted away under their feet, continue to vegetate as their heirs begin to quarrel over their claims to the inheritance — even before the obituary notice has been printed and the testament unsealed; and it is an old maxim, borne out by history, that before their final death agony these social forces summon up their strength once more and move from the defensive to the offensive, issuing challenges instead of giving ground, and attempting to draw the most extreme conclusions from premises which have not only been called into question but have already been condemned. Such is the case today with the English oligarchy: and such is the case with its twin sister, the Church. There have been innumerable attempts at reorganization within the Established Church, both High and Low, and attempts to come to terms with the dissenters so that the profane masses can be confronted with a compact force. Measures of religious coercion have followed each other in rapid succession — in the House of Lords the pious Lord Ashley bewailed the fact that in England alone five million people had become estranged not only from the Church but from Christianity. The Established Church replies, *Compelle intrare*. It leaves it to Lord Ashley and similar dissenting, sectarian and hysterical pietists to pull out of the fire the chestnuts which it intends to eat itself.

The Beer Bill, which closed all places of public amusement on Sundays except between six and ten p.m., was the first example of religious coercion. It was smuggled through a sparsely attended House at the end of a sitting, after the pietists had bought the support of the larger London publicans by guaranteeing them the continuation of the licensing system — the continued monopoly of big capital. Then came the Sunday Trading Bill, which has now passed its third reading in the Commons and which has just been debated clause by clause by the Committee of the Whole House. In this new coercive measure, too, the interest of big capital has been heeded, as only small shopkeepers do business on Sundays and the big shops are quite willing to eliminate the Sunday competition of the by parliamentary means. In both cases we find a conspiracy between the Church and the capitalist monopolies, and in both religious penal laws aimed at the lower classes to set at rest the conscience of the privileged classes. The aristocratic clubs were no more hit by the Beer Bill than the Sunday occupations of fashionable society an the Sunday Trading Bill. The working class receives its wages on Saturdays; Sunday trading, therefore, exists solely for them. They are the only section of the population forced to make their small purchases on Sundays, and the new bill is directed against them all. In the Eighteenth Century the French aristocracy said, "For us, Voltaire; for the people, mass and tithes." In the Nineteenth Century the English aristocracy says, "For us pious phrases; for the people, Christian practice." The classical saints of Christianity mortified their bodies to save the souls of the masses; the modern, educated saints mortify the *bodies of the masses* to save their own souls.

This alliance between a degenerate, dissipated and pleasure-seeking aristocracy and the Church — built on a foundation of filthy and calculated profiteering on the part of monopolistic wholesalers — gave rise to a *mass demonstration* in Hyde Park yesterday, such as London has not seen since the death of George IV, the "first gentleman of Europe." We witnessed the event from beginning to end and believe we can state without exaggeration that *yesterday in Hyde Park the English revolution began.* The latest news from the Crimea acted as an important ferment in this *"unparliamentary," "extra-parliamentary"* and *"anti-parliamentary"* demonstration.

The instigator of the Sunday Trading Bill, Lord Robert Grosvenor, had answered the objection that his bill was directed only against the poor and not against the rich classes by saying that the aristocracy was largely refraining from employing its servants and horses on Sundays. At the end of last week the following poster issued *by the Chartists* could be seen on all the walls in London announcing in large print:

> *New Sunday Bill* prohibiting newspapers, shaving, smoking, eating and drinking and all other kinds of recreation and nourishment both corporal and spiritual, which the *poor people* still enjoy at the present time. *An open-air meeting* of artisans, workers and *"the lower orders"* generally of the capital will take place in Hyde Park on Sunday afternoon to see how religiously the aristocracy is observing the Sabbath and how anxious it is not to employ its servants and horses on that day, as Lord Robert Grosvenor said in his speech. The meeting is called for three o'clock on the right bank of the Serpentine, on the side towards Kensington Gardens. Come and bring your wives and children in order that they may profit by the example their "betters" set them!

It should be realized that what Longchamps means to the Parisians, the road along the Serpentine means to English high society; it is the place where in the afternoons, particularly on Sundays, they parade their magnificent carriages with all their trappings and exercise their horses followed by swarms of lackeys. It will be evidence from the poster quoted above that the struggle against clericalism, like every serious struggle in England, is assuming the character of a *class struggle* waged by the poor against the rich, by the people against the aristocracy, by the "lower orders" against their "betters."

At 3 o'clock about fifty thousand people had gathered at the appointed spot on the right bank of the Serpentine in the huge meadows of Hyde Park. Gradually the numbers swelled to at least two hundred thousand as people came from the left bank too. Small knots of people could be seen being jostled from one spot to another. A large contingent of police was evidently attempting to deprive the organizers of the meeting of what Archimedes had demanded in order to move the earth: a fixed place to stand on. Finally, a large crowd made a firm stand and the Chartist (James) Bligh constituted himself chairman on a small rise in the middle of the crowd. No sooner had he begun to harangue than Police Inspector Banks at the head of forty truncheon-swinging constables explained to him that the Park was the private property of the Crown and that they were not allowed to hold a meeting in it. After some preliminary exchanges in the course of which Bligh tried to demonstrate that the Park was public property and Banks replied that he had strict orders to arrest him if he persisted in his intention, Bligh shouted amidst the tremendous roar of the masses around him: "Her Majesty's police declare that Hyde Park is the private property of the Crown and that Her Majesty is not inclined to lend her land to the people for their meetings. So let us adjourn to Oxford Market."

With the ironic cry of "*God save the Queen!*" the throng dispersed in the direction of Oxford Market. But meanwhile (James) Finlen, a member of the Chartist leadership, had rushed to a tree some distance away. A crowd followed him and surrounded him instantly in such a tight and compact circle that the police abandoned their attempts to force their way through to him. "We are enslaved for six days a week," he said, "and Parliament wants to rob us of our bit of freedom on the seventh. These oligarchs and capitalists and their allies, the sanctimonious clerics, want to do *penance* — not by mortifying themselves but by mortifying us — for the unconscionable murder committed against the sons of the people sacrificed in the Crimea."

We left this group to approach another where a speaker, stretched out on the ground, was haranguing his audience from this horizontal position. Suddenly from all sides came the cry: "Let's go to the road. Let's go to the carriages." Meanwhile people had already begun heaping insults on the carriages and riders. The constables, who were steadily receiving reinforcements, drove the pedestrians back from the road. They thus helped to form a dense avenue of people on either side which extended for more than a quarter of an hour's walk from Aspley House, up Rotten Row, and along the Serpentine as far as Kensington Gardens. The public gathering consisted of about two-thirds workers and one-third members of the middle class, all with their wives and children. The reluctant actors — elegant gentle men and ladies, "commoners and lords" in high coaches-and-four with liveried servants in front and behind, elderly gentlemen alone on horseback, a little flushed from their port wine — this time did not pass by in review. They ran the gauntlet. A babel of jeering, taunting and discordant noises — in which no language is so rich as the English — soon closed in upon them from all sides. As the concert was improvised there was a lack of instrumental accompaniment. The chorus, therefore, had to make use of its own organs and to confine itself to vocal music. And what a diabolical concert it was: a cacophony of grunting, hissing, whistling, squawking, snarling, growling, croaking, yelling, groaning, rattling, shrieking, gnashing sounds. Music to drive a man out of his mind, music to move a stone. Added to this came outbursts of genuine Old English humour strangely mixed with boiling and long-constrained anger. "Go to church!" was the only recognizable articulate sound. In a conciliatory fashion one lady stretched out an orthodoxly-bound prayerbook from the coach. "Give it to your horses to read!" the thunder of a thousand voices echoed back. When the horses shied, reared, bucked and bolted, endangering the lives of their elegant burdens, the mocking cries became louder, more menacing, more implacable. Noble lords and ladies, among them Lady Granville, wife of the President of the Privy Council, were forced to alight and make use of their feet. When elderly gentlemen rode by whose dress — in particular the broad-brimmed hat — evinced a special claim to purity of faith, all the sounds of fury were extinguished, at a command — by inextinguishable laughter. One of these gentlemen lost his patience. Like Mephistopheles he made an indecent gesture: he stuck his tongue out at the enemy. "He is a wordcatcher! a parliamentary man! He fights with his own weapons!" some one called out from one side of the road. "He is a saint! he is psalm singing!" came the antistrophe from the other side.

Meanwhile the metropolitan electric telegraph had announced to all police stations that a riot was imminent in Hyde Park and ordered the police to the theatre of war. So at short intervals one police detachment after another marched between the two rows of people from Aspley House to Kensington Garden, each being met with the popular ditty:

Where are the geese?
Ask the police!

This refers to a notorious theft of geese which a constable recently committed in Clerkenwell.

The spectacle lasted for three hours. Only English lungs are capable of such a feat. During the performance opinions such as "This is only the beginning!" "This is the first step!" "We hate them!" etc. could be heard from various groups. While hatred could be read in the faces of the workers we have never seen such smug, self-satisfied smiles as those that covered the faces of the middle classes. Just before the end the demonstration increased in violence. Sticks were shaken at the carriages, and through the endless discordant din the cry could be heard: "You rascals!" Zealous Chartist men and women battled their way through the crowds throughout these three hours, distributing leaflets which declared in large type:

> *Reorganization of Chartism*! A big public meeting will take place next Tuesday, 26 June, in the Literary and Scientific Institute in Friar Street, Doctor's Commons, to elect delegates to a conference for the reorganization of Chartism in the capital. Admission free.

Today's London papers carry on average only a short account of the events in Hyde Park. There have been no leading articles yet with the exception of Lord Palmerston's *Morning Post*. This paper writes:

> A scene, in the highest degree disgraceful and dangerous, was enacted yesterday in Hyde Park... (an) outrage on law and decency... It was distinctly illegal to interfere, by physical force, in the free action of the legislature... We must have no repetition of violence on Sunday next, as has been threatened.

But at the same time it declares that the "fanatical" Lord Grosvenor is solely responsible for the trouble and that he has provoked the "just indignation of the people!" As if Parliament has not given Lord Grosvenor's Bill its three readings! Has he perhaps also exerted pressure "by physical force in the free action of the legislature?"

London, 2nd July.

The demonstration against the Sunday Bill was repeated in Hyde Park yesterday on a larger scale, under a more ominous sign and with more serious consequences, as it witnessed by the sombre but agitated mood in London today.

The posters calling for the repetition of the meeting also contained an invitation to assemble on Sunday at 10 a.m. before the house of the pious Lord Grosvenor and to accompany him to church. The pious gentleman, however, had left London on Saturday in a private carriage — in order to travel incognito. That he is by nature destined to make martyrs of others rather than to be a martyr himself had been demonstrated by his circular in all the London newspapers, in which he on the one hand upheld his Bill and on the other took pains to show that it is without meaning, function or significance. On Sunday his house was occupied all day not by psalm singers but by constables, two hundred in number. Such was the case, too, at the house of his brother, the Marquess of Westminster, a man famous for his wealth.

On Saturday the head of the London police, Sir Richard Mayne, had posters stuck on all the walls in London in which he *"prohibited"* not only a meeting in Hyde Park but also the gathering of any "large numbers" and the manifestation of any signs of approval or disapproval. The result of these decrees was that as early as 3 o'clock — even according to the report of the *Police Gazette* — one hundred and fifty thousand people of every age and social position were milling about. Gradually the crowds swelled to gigantic proportions unbelievable even by London standards. Not only did London appear *en masse*; an avenue of spectators formed again on both sides of the road along the Serpentine; only this time the crowd was denser and deeper than last Sunday. High society, however, stayed away. Altogether perhaps twenty vehicles put in an appearance, most of them gigs and phaetons, which drove by without hindrance. Their more stately and better upholstered brethren, who displayed larger paunches and more livery, were greeted with the old shouts and with the old babel of noise; and this time the sound waves made the air vibrate for at least a mile around. The police decrees were given a rebuttal by the mass gathering and by the chorus of noise from a thousand throats. High society had avoided the field of battle and by its absence it had acknowledged the sovereignty of the *vox populi*.

It was 4 o'clock. The demonstration seemed to be fizzling out into a harmless Sunday outing for want of any combustible elements. But the police had other plans. Were they to withdraw to the accompaniment of general laughter, casting wistful parting glances at their own posters, which could be read in large print at the entrance to the park? Besides, their high dignitaries were present: Sir Richard Mayne and Superintendents Gibbs and Walker on horseback, Inspectors Banks, Darkin and Brennan on foot. Eight hundred constables had been strategically deployed, for the most part hidden in buildings and concealed in ambush. Stronger detachments had been stationed in neighbouring districts as reinforcements. At a point of intersection where the road along the Serpentine crosses a path leading towards Kensington Gardens, the Ranger's Lodge, the Magazine and the premises of the Royal Humane Society had been transformed into improvised blockhouses manned by a strong police contingent; each building had been prepared to accommodate prisoners and wounded. Cabs stood at the ready at the police station in Vine Street, Piccadilly, waiting to drive to the scene of battle and to take away the defeated demonstrators under safe escort. In short, the police had drawn up a plan of campaign "more vigorous," as *The Times* said, "than any of which we have yet had notice in the Crimea." The police needed bloody heads and arrests so as not to stumble straight from the sublime into the ridiculous. So, as soon as the avenue of spectators had cleared somewhat, and the masses had dispersed away from the road into different groups on the huge expanse of the park, their senior officers took up positions in the middle of the road, between the rows of people, and from their horses they issued pompous orders right and left, supposedly for the protection of the carriages and horsemen passing by.

As there were no carriages or horsemen, however, and therefore nothing to protect, they began to pick out individuals from the crowd "on false pretexts" and to have them arrested on the pretext that they were pickpockets. As these experiments increased in number and the pretext lost its credibility the crowds raised a general cry, and the contingents of police broke out from their hiding places. Drawing their truncheons from their pockets they beat heads bloody, tore people out of the crowd here and there — altogether there were one hundred and four such arrests — and dragged them to the improvised blockhouses. The left side of the road is separated only by a narrow piece of ground from the Serpentine. By manoeuvring his gang of constables a police officer managed to drive the spectators close to the edge of the water, where he threatened them with a cold bath. In order to escape the police truncheons one man swam across the Serpentine to the other bank; a policeman gave chase in a boat, caught him and brought him back in triumph.

How the scene had changed since the previous Sunday! Instead of elegant coaches-and-four, dirty cabs, which drove back and forth between the police station at Vine Street and the improvised jails in Hyde Park. Instead of lackeys on the boxes of carriages, constables sitting next to drunken cab drivers. Inside the vehicles, instead of elegant gentlemen and ladies, prisoners with bloody heads, dishevelled hair, half-undressed and with torn clothes, guarded by dubious conscripts from the Irish *lumpenprotelariat* who had been pressed into the London police. Instead of the wafting of fans, a hail of truncheons. Last Sunday the ruling classes had shown their fashionable face; this time the face they displayed was that of the state. In the background — behind the affably grinning old gentlemen, the fashionable dandies, the elegantly infirm widows and the perfumed beauties in their cashmeres, ostrich feathers, and garlands of flowers and diamonds — stood the constable with his waterproof coat, greasy oilskin hat and truncheon — the reverse side of the coin. Last Sunday the ruling classes had confronted the masses as individuals. This time they assumed the form of state power, law and truncheon. This time resistance amounted to insurrection, and the Englishman must be subjected to long slow provocation before he is moved to insurrection. Thus, the counter-demonstration was limited, on the whole, to hissing, grunting and whistling at the police vehicles, to isolated attempts to free the prisoners but, above all, to passive resistance, as the crowds phlegmatically stood their ground on the field of battle.

Soldiers — partly from the Guard, partly from the Sixty-Sixth Regiment - assumed a characteristic role in this spectacle. They had appeared in force. Twelve of them, some decorated with medals from the Crimea stood among a group of men, women and children on whom the police truncheons were descending. An old man fell to the ground, struck by a blow. "The London stiffstaffs" (a term of abuse for the police) "are worse than the Russians at Inkerman," called out one of the

Crimean heroes. The police seized him. He was immediately freed to the accompaniment of shouts from the crowd: "Three cheers for the army!" The police deemed it advisable to move off. Meanwhile, a number of Grenadiers had arrived; the soldiers fell into line and with the crowd milling about them shouting, "Hurrah for the army, down with the police, down with the Sunday Bill," they paraded up and down in the park. The police stood about irresolutely, when a sergeant of the Guard appeared and loudly called them to account for their brutality, calmed the soldiers and persuaded some of them to follow him to the barracks to avoid more serious collisions. But the majority of the soldiers remained behind, and from among the people they gave vent to their anger at the police in no uncertain terms. In England the opposition between the police and the army is an old one. The present moment, when the army is the "pet child" of the masses, is certainly not likely to reduce this opposition.

An old man named Russell is said to have died today as a result of the wounds he suffered yesterday; half a dozen people are in St George's hospital suffering from injuries. During the demonstration different attempts were again made to hold smaller meetings, In one of them, near the Albert Gate outside the section of the park originally occupied by the police, an anonymous speaker harangued his public something like this:

> Men of Old England! Awake, rise up from your slumber or fall for ever; resist the government every Sunday! Observe the Sunday Bill as you have done today. Do not be afraid to demand those rights to which you are entitled. Cast off the fetters of oligarchical oppression and tyranny. If you do not, you will be hopelessly crushed. Is it not outrageous that the inhabitants of this great metropolis, the greatest in the civilised world, must surrender their freedom into the hands of a Lord Grosvenor or a man like Lord Ebrington! His Lordship feels obliged to drive us to Church and to make us religious by means of an act of Parliament. His attempts are in vain. Who are we, and who are they? Look at the war which is being fought. Is it not being waged at the expense and with the blood of the productive classes? And what about the unproductive class? They have bungled it from start to finish.

Speaker and meeting were, of course, interrupted by the police.

In Greenwich, near the Observatory, Londoners also held a meeting of ten to fifteen thousand people, which was likewise broken up by the police.

Ben Tillet

The Hyde Park Railway to Reform

Royden Harrison

Royden Harrison was formerly Reader in Political Theory and Institutions at Sheffield University and is now professor of social history at the University of Warwick. In 1960 he was the co-founder and has remained the co-editor of the *Bulletin* of the Society for the Study of Labour History. He is also a member of the editorial board of the *Political Quarterly* and of the advisory boards of *Victorian Studies* and *Tribune*. His principal published work is *Before the Socialists: Studies in Labour and Politics, 1861-1881* (1965). He has been commissioned by the Passfield trustees to write the life of Sidney and Beatrice Webb. He was the first president of the Socialist Charter and has frequently addressed the Labour Party Conference as the delegate of the Sheffield (Hallam) Constituency Labour Party. In 1970 and 1971 he stood for the Labour Party's National Executive Committee, obtaining well over one hundred thousand votes on each occasion.

THE "Great" Reform Act of 1832 ended the rule of "Old Corruption" and conferred increased power upon the landed gentry and the urban middle class. Bertrand Russell's grandfather, Lord John Russell, declared that this must be regarded as a final measure of Reform. Alas for "Finality Jack!" Demands for a further extension of the franchise continued to agitate British politics for the next 30 years. Until 1848 the demand came mainly from "without": the Chartists held the field. After 1848 "Reform" was reintroduced into parliamentary politics and there was a succession of abortive Reform Bills: in 1852, 1854, 1859 and 1860.

Before 1848 Reform was not carried because it would have been too dangerous to concede it. After 1848 it was not conceded because the House of Commons was too comfortable to move. The House was ready to take up Reform as a subject for petty party manoeuvres, but such manoeuvres never caught the imagination of the people. It was not until 1866-7 that Reform became the decisive question both within Parliament and out of doors. The success of the post-Chartist agitation lay in the manner in which it exhibited a number of contradictory characteristics. It was these characteristics which made it dangerous for the ruling classes to resist Reform and safe for them to concede it.

Despite important continuities, the British Labour movement in the third quarter of the Nineteenth Century looked very different from what it had done in the second. Co-operation abandoned community building in favour of shop-keeping and exchanged the new moral world for "the divi." Trade unionism became less of a school of war and more of a workman's equivalent of the public school. From aspiring to the control of industry, it limited itself to attempting to control the supply of labour. Its new leaders taught it, not militancy, but how to be respectable and respected: to practise, not the class war, but industry, chastity and sobriety.

Labour leaders themselves ceased to be inspired "outsiders"; visionaries and demagogues: Robert Owen: Bronterre O'Brien: Fergus O'Connor. They were increasingly "insiders": products of the new Labour bureaucracies: great men of business: Allan of the Engineers: Applegarth of the Carpenters and Joiners.

The very rhythm of the Labour movement changed. Whereas it had advanced most markedly during the troughs in the trade cycle, after 1850 new departures tended to be associated with the upswing in the cycle. Throughout the second quarter of the century organised Labour had generally been open to dreams of a total reconstruction of existing society. During the third quarter its concern became more with securing its own incorporation within that society.

These large changes in attitudes and institutions have to be understood in relation to the altered composition of the working classes The fiercest and most turbulent element in Chartism had been supplied, not by the artisans nor by the factory operatives, but by the depressed domestic outworkers: handloom weavers and framework knitters who were being extinguished by the competition of machine industry.

After 1850 the skilled engineers and the relatively privileged aristocrats of Labour ceased to be despised as "pukes" or "exclusives" and took the place of the domestic outworkers as the stratum which set the tone and the pace for the Labour movement as a whole. The new institutions presupposed the presence of this relatively privileged stratum. The Co-operative store which refused credit and the trade union which was built on high contributions and high benefits effectively shut out the great mass of the labouring population.

This new Labour movement which attained maturity in the 1860's was both frightening and reassuring to the propertied classes. It was reassuring to have a working class whose leaders boasted that their people were themselves becoming capitalists. In a society which lacked a peasantry it was comforting to think that part of the working class was acquiring a stake in the country and learning the corporate management of vast sums of money through the unions and the Co-ops. It was agreeable to have workmen who wanted the vote, not as a hammer to knock property on the head, but as a means of rising in the social scale.

When Mr. Gladstone was reproached by one of his aristocratic relatives with encouraging the demand for Reform he replied: "Please to recollect that we have got to govern millions of hard hands. That it must be done by force, fraud, or good will. That the latter has been tried and is answering, that none have profited more by this change of system since the Corn Law and the Six Acts than those who complain of it."

There were plenty of men who understood the conservative possibilities of democracy. Provided the mere labourers, the dangerous classes, the "residuum" could be excluded, there was not too much to fear. The power of property was recognised to depend less upon privileged access to political decision-taking than upon "those occult and unacknowledged forces that are not dependent upon any legislative machinery." In other words, upon the power of deference. Upon the readiness of a substantial number of working men to look upon the world of the gay and splendid not with a jealous envy, but with admiration.

The trouble was that the skilled workmen did not claim to speak for themselves alone. They demanded manhood suffrage and vote by ballot. In practice, they showed a greater readiness to settle for the half loaf than the Chartists had done. But they were much more perfectly organised.

The Reform League which numbered its members in over six hundred branches was the most complete political machine that had yet been created. If this League was ready to co-operate with middle-class radicals, as the Chartists had not been ready to, it nevertheless insisted upon own organisational and programatic independence. If it had given up the vision of working-class ascendancy it was determined upon securing political equality. If Parliament continued to trifle with the question of Reform then there was every reason to believe that the workers would display an increasing contempt for authority and would become more and more unmanageable. This is evident from the progress of the Reform agitation which may be seen to have passed through three major stages in terms of its relationship to established power.

In the spring of 1866 the Russell-Gladstone administration introduced a Reform Bill. It was such a limited measure that it failed to inspire any public enthusiasm. However, it went far enough to alarm the most reactionary Whigs. They succeeded in bringing the Government down. A minority Tory administration led by Derby and Disraeli took its place.

These developments aroused Reformers in the country. The Reform League announced its intention of holding a mass meeting in Hyde Park. When the police closed the gates against the crowd the pressure on the railings caused them to give way. For three days and nights rioting occurred. John Stuart Mill described how he had to use all his persuasive powers to induce the Labour leaders to avoid a revolutionary confrontation. In the end the Home Secretary, powerless to restore order without his help, had to enlist the assistance of Beales, the President of the League, so as to clear the park.

The next stage was reached in the winter of 1866-7. There was an outbreak of cholera in London and unemployment was rising at the same time as the price of bread was increasing. The legal status of trade unions was being called into question by decisions in the courts and by the establishment of a Royal Commission. The metropolitan police advised the Government that it could no longer guarantee the maintenance of order if massive Reform demonstrations were permitted in London. The response of the League was to project the creation of its own Reform constabulary. The middle-class Radical leader, John Bright, was seriously alarmed and suggested that if this were done the country would find itself on a soil "hot with volcanic fire." Mill, finding himself unable to dissuade the League leaders from dangerous courses, ended his association with them.

In February 1867 Disraeli began to venture along the tortuous parliamentary path that led to Reform. By April his Bill appeared to be making little headway. At this point the League resolved to assert once more the right of public meeting in Hyde Park. The Government banned the meeting and concentrated troops in and around the park. It mobilised thousands of special constables. Men were employed on overtime making batons. Police officers descended on the offices of the Reform League threatening the direst consequences if the authority of the Government was challenged. There were rumours that artillery was being brought into London from Aldershot. Beales, under heavy pressure from his own left wing, refused to be intimidated.

On the evening of May 6, 1867, the Reform League called the Tory bluff. A vast army of Reformers marched triumphantly through the gates and occupied the park. Whereas in July 1866 the Government had been unable to maintain order without the League, in May 1867 the orders of the League prevailed over those of the Government.

The middle-class press could not conceal its anguish. The "roughs" had triumphed over respectable society. It was evident that the Reform question would have to be brought to a conclusion as soon as possible. The Prime Minister himself was forced to acknowledge that his Administration had "suffered some slight humiliation in the public mind." He offered up his luckless Home Secretary, Spencer Walpole, as a sacrifice. The victory of the Reform League on May 6th, 1867, had revenged the humiliation of the Chartists on April 10, 1848. The League was henceforth a power. It exchanged messages with Bismarck and enrolled Garibaldi among its members. Its class pride was enormously enhanced. It adopted a sharp and censorious tone in its dealing with those *bourgeois* patrons to whom it had hitherto tended to defer.

Gladstone had advised the League against a confrontation with the Government. He now moved sharply to the left. Disraeli had already privately revealed his own motives: he sought, he explained, "to destroy the present agitation and to extinguish Gladstone and Co." He could only hope to attain the second of these objectives to the extent that he was able to convince Parliament that it was imperative to achieve the first. The "destruction" of the agitation was only possible through far-reaching concessions to its demands: concessions which went far beyond anything which Disraeli, Gladstone, Bright or any other Parliamentarian had wanted or imagined. Dizzy had, at all costs, to avoid appearing to accept dictation from his great rival. Under the circumstances he could only do so by accepting amendments still more radical than those favoured by the Liberal leader.

Disraeli had little interest or knowledge of the details of the Bill. He was probably tiddly for a good deal of the time. He asked his colleagues to come and speak on key clauses explaining that he did not care whether they spoke for or against so long as they spoke. But behind a pleasant alcoholic haze, the mind was clear: he was going to stay on the horse's back even if he could not pretend to determine just how far the horse was going to go. And it did not go all that far: before Reform one adult male in five had the vote: after Reform the proportion was still only one in three.

When the Government surrendered to the League on May 6th, it exchanged the associations of Peterloo for those of Hyde Park. Henceforth Hyde Park acquired its distinctive significance within the British political tradition. It stood for the triumph of popular rights over aristocratic enthusiasm before those "occult and unacknowledged forces that are not dependent upon any legislative machinery." The limitations of the right that had been established are as evident as the right itself.

As with the park, so with Reform. The workers were encroaching on established power and simultaneously being involved more deeply in the status quo. The very advance that they made diminished their own sense of identity upon which further advance depended. Within the framework of the liberal democratic state it was to prove difficult to recover the spirit of "the Democracy" — the rule of all the poor and all the oppressed. The workers had to master a new kind of politics once "good will" had been tried and was answering.

References for "The Hyde Park Railway to Reform"

Royden Harrison: *Before the Socialists: Studies in Labour and Politics in England, 1861-1881* (1965) The present article derives from the third chapter of this book.

Henry Katz: *Anglia U Progu Demarkracji* (England on the Threshold of Democracy), (Warsaw, 1965) This scholarly and important work badly needs to find an English translation; the same applies to Dr. Katz's monograph history of the Reform League.

F. B. Smith: *The Making of the Second Reform Bill* (Cambridge, 1966) The best general history available, sound, balanced and reliable if not inspired.

Maurice Cowling: *1867, Disraeli, Gladstone and Revolution* (Cambridge, 1967), pp. 450. Originally a polemical attack on the chapter referred to above in Harrison: written from the standpoint of "pure" and "high" politics.

Gertrude Himmelfarb: *Victorian Minds* (1968) The last chapter is a furious assault on Whig, Marxist and the new left dogs barking in the gutter. More entertaining but perhaps less responsible than Cowling.

F. M. Leventhal: *Respectable Radical* (1971). A careful biography of George Flowell, the Secretary of the Reform League.

Tom Mann and His Times (excerpt)

Dona Torr

"GOADED by the attacks of the Socialists and New Trade Unionists," records George Howell, the London Trades Council found itself obliged to participate in "May day celebrations in favour of the 'solidarity of labour,' Eight Hours and other idealistic proposals." (*Trade Unionism old and New*, 1891, pp. 191-7).

May day demonstrations for the legal 8-hour day, resolved upon by the foundation congress of the Second International (July, 1889), took place in 1890 in the U.S.A. and in all the chief European countries, to the dismay of the ruling classes. Amid the general excitement provoked by press accounts of preparations on the continent and arrests in Paris, *Punch*, whose cartoons had already depicted haggard men about to destroy the Goose that Lays the Golden Eggs, or to sew tares from a basket labelled Socialism, or to step into an abyss labelled Anarchy, now portrayed "The New Queen of the May!" with a bomb in one hand, a lily in the other, a sash labelled "International," and garlands labelled "Eight Hours," "Strikes," "Agitations," "Solidarity," "Dynamite"; but, perhaps as an antidote to continentalism, also printed some lolloping sympathetic lines (April 30th, 1890):

> They've kept us scattered till now, comrade; but that no more may be;
> Our shout goes up in unison by Thames, Seine, Rhine and Spree.
> We are not the crushed down crowd, chummy, we were but yesterday;
> We're full of the Promise O' May, brother; mad with the promise of May.

Eleanor Marx and Edward Aveling had initiated in the London east end an agitation which had first introduced English workers to the new Socialist International whose foundation congress John Burns had attended. To carry out the eight hour day resolution they had organised the Central Committee for the Eight Hours Legal Working Day Demonstration, first parent of London's later May Day Committee. To them we owe our first London May Day, its international tradition then begun, and the grandeur of the demonstration. The participation of the thirty-year-old London Trades Council, representing mainly the old crafts but now including in its procession the dockers we owe chiefly to Tom Mann. By proposing a separate demonstration organised by the council he made it possible to overcome the difficulties arising from the invitation of the Central Committee and the dread word "legal." At the delegate meeting on April 10th he moved: "that this council of delegates recommend the trade societies of the metropolis to demonstrate in favour of an eight hours working day." This having been carried, he seconded Drummond's motion that a demonstration should be organised by the Trades Council on May 4th.[1]

To Burns, who was supporting the Central Committee, Tom wrote on April 30th with some anxiety:

> Respecting the Trades Council position, re 8 hours. They have decided on a resolution drawn up by myself, and afterwards slightly modified, to the effect that we strive to bring about the 8 hours "by every legitimate means'" and call upon Government to at once start the same in Government Department. I shall be Chairman of the Central Platform provided by the T.C. and I shall urge the importance of Trade Union action as a means of education up to the demanding of better conditions; I sincerely hope that your speech and mine will be on the same lines; I shall not of course insist on any sweeping measures as that I am sure is impossible. More and more I am convinced of the impudence of men like Graham, there has been no talk about pledging ourselves to individual effort such as Graham talks about. I suppose you have definitely promised to speak on the platform of the Aveling section. If so, it would be policy to emphasise the importance of Trade Unionism. Large numbers would like to find you and I advocating different methods. If you have any special recommendation let me have it, please, and I will comply. I have endeavoured to state the case in May number of *Nineteenth Century* and should like your opinion upon it; I don't know what I shall get for it but I shall hand over the cheque towards the £35 *Elector* account...
>
> There is no serious difference between the Legalists and L.T.C., we are providing seven platforms and giving one of them to S.D.F. to appoint their own speaker etc.: they have now asked that we provide a second and they will pay for it, So we shall do so; I am on the Sub-Committee making arrangements. It has so upset Ben he has gone to Bournemouth for a day or two. I was at Full last week and had good meetings ...

Harmonious joint arrangements having been achieved (not without some trouble from George Shipton, secretary of the Trades Council, who made a prior booking of Hyde Park which nearly excluded the Avelings' section) the council had its separate procession, platforms and resolution. Both processions assembled at the same time on the embankment, the Trades Council on the river side, the Central Committee on the north side of the roadway, they then marched by separate routes to the park

---

[1] *L.T.C. Minutes*, see also *London Trades Council*, p. 76

where each had seven platforms, the Trades Council north and south of the Reformer's Tree and the Central Committee parallel with these by Broad walk.[1]

Thus in the eyes of the deeply impressed public, the demonstration of Sunday, May 4th, 1890 — the processions which took over two hours to file into the park, the crowd which finally totalled half a million[2] — was a single demonstration for the eight hour-day, a revelation of the new "idealistic" independence and solidarity of the working class. Fred Henderson wrote in next day's *Star*:

> We toilers of the field and town
> By long oppression trodden down
> In every clime beneath the sun
> Have seen the new life to be won;
> Seen that all the strife we waged
> Was but fool with fool engaged:
> Where we erst as foemen stood
> Lo, to-day reigns brotherhood.

George Shipton was Chief Marshall of the Trades Council procession, in which the dockers, despised outcasts eight months before, now marched "in their rough working clothes" together with the ancient aristocracy: "sandwiched" between them, as the *Star* recorded were "hundreds of gentlemen comps, kid-gloved and top-hatted." No such demonstration in Hyde Park had been seen since 1866; "in point of numbers the most remarkable ever held in London[3]." Every feature excited comment: the novel "small shield shaped banners" with white letters on crimson backgrounds marking, the sections of the Central committee's procession, and the "acres of splendidly painted silk" carried by the unions. "Along both routes the classes came out to see the masses," reported the *Star* next day. "The balconies of the great houses... were crowded with ladies and gentlemen of the upper ten thousand. From the upper windows the servants looked on."

Tom Mann had been given the task of marshalling east end workers, not attached to any particular organisation, who were joining the demonstration[4]. After marshalling some thousands of "unattached men" on the embankment with the help of two "mounted farriers" Tom, wearing his President's blue sash of the Dockers' Union, was chairman of the main Trades Council platform, from which the resolution was moved by Ben Tillett. Tom's support for the full socialist demand of a legal eight-hour-day was well enough known, his second pamphlet on the subject, *The Eight Hours Movement* (1889) was just then selling widely,

---

[1] *Reynolds's Newspaper*, May 4, 1890.
[2] *Star*, May 5, 1890
[3] *Reynolds's* May 11th, 1890
[4] *Star*, May 1st

but he spoke loyally to the Trades Council resolution which only recommended getting an eight-hour-day "by every legitimate means in their power." The resolution, *Reynolds's* noted (May 21th) "went quite as far as was judicious for the Council"; the fact that they were met under the auspices of the Council showed that this body "which some thought lethargic, was now making progress."

Tom's platform, well surrounded by dockers, railwaymen, barge builders and rope makers, was the only Trades Council platform which drew a crowd. By far the greatest masses were gathered round the platforms of the Central Committee, where the speakers included John Burns, Will Thorne, John Ward, Cunninghame Graham, Bernard Shaw, Stepniak, Paul Lafargue and the Avelings. Burns, amid cheers, flung out his challenge to Bradlaugh: if they both spoke to an audience of two hundred thousand he could still win ninety per cent of it for the legal eight-hour day. Four branches of the S.D.F. marched with the Central Committee and the S.D.F. had its two platforms near the Trades Council; their resolution added the demand for socialist ownership to that of the legal eight-hour-day.

"What would I give if Marx had lived to see this awakening!" was Engel's first thought as he watched the great scene from the roof of a vehicle. "I held my head two inches higher when I climbed down from the old goods van[1]." Great though the success had been in other countries, he wrote later in an article in the *Vienna Arbeiterzeitung* (May 23rd, 1890), the grandest and most important part of the whole May Day festival was that: "On 4 May 1890, the English proletariat, newly awakened from its forty years winter sleep, again entered the movement of its class... The grandchildren of the old Chartists are entering the line of battle."

---

[1] Gustave Mayer, *Friedrich Engels*, 1936, p. 253

Tom Mann

The First London May Day (excerpt)

The Star
Eric J. Hobsbawm (Ed.)

IT seemed as though the whole population of London poured parkwards... One thing the processions demonstrated was the way in which all classes of the workers join hands on the eight hours. There were dockers there in their rough working clothes — the only clothes they have probably — and sandwiched between them hundreds of gentlemen comps, kid-gloved and top-hatted. One spirit animated them all...

From [the Reformers' Tree] one could see both the Marble Arch and Hyde Park Corner, and the great tract of lawn between. Before the processions arrived there were a few thousand people about, looking nothing in the vast space, and round each entrance a thicker crowd waiting to see the processions enter. But when the stream set in by both gates, the black group at each corner began to grow and spread out fan-like over the open space, advancing like great waves up into the Park until the grass was swallowed up and the only prospect was people thick-thronged everywhere ... and all the time the procession was still coming in. There was the banner of the Postmen's Union... A slight break and up came the dockers, an interminable array with multitudinous banners ... Then came a large contingent of women — rope makers, match-makers and others. Looked at from above they advanced like a moving rainbow, for they all wore the huge feathers of many colours which the East End lass loves to sport when she is out for the day...

Militant Suffragettes (excerpt)

Antonia Raeburn

"WOMEN'S Sunday" in Hyde Park was to be the greatest franchise demonstration ever known. Pethick-Lawrence had devised the scheme to prove that the women's movement held overwhelming public support. No cost was spared and detailed plans were made for accommodating the vast crowds expected at the meeting. To prevent a recurrence of the 1886 franchise rioting when the park railings were torn down, Pethick-Lawrence arranged with the authorities to have some of the railings temporarily removed.

Four months before the demonstration was to take place, the staff at Clement's Inn began work on a publicity campaign. Mrs. Tuke, known as Pansy, was an Honorable Secretary on the W.S.P.U.[1] committee and her social assets were invaluable in the normal running of the office. Now she was caught up in the general upheaval and she wrote to Isabel Seymour somewhat distractedly: "You would hardly know the place if you came into it now, a regular hive of busy people jostling and pushing. Two more large rooms have been taken on the ground floor..." The Pethick-Lawrences engaged extra help and five thousand pounds was set aside for advertising alone.

There were to be eighty women speakers and twenty platforms in the park. Early in the campaign a "Record Poster" appeared on hoardings throughout the country with life-size portraits of the twenty women chairmen, and handbills were circulated giving details of the seven processions that were to converge on the park from various parts of London. Railway excursions were arranged to bring parties from the provinces, and a quarter of a million mock train tickets were printed to encourage people to make use of the special transport. In London W.S.P.U. canvassers went to factories, shops, hospitals and restaurants, calling on working women to join them. "Bring your friends and family to Hyde Park, and you must wear the colours."

Purple, white and green, symbolising justice, purity and hope, had been chosen by Mrs. Lawrence to represent the movement. Articles in the colours were soon on sale, and picture hats and baby bonnets could be bought with trimmings stamped "Votes for Women." The Women's Press stocked striped shantung motor scarves printed with the Suffragette motto, and tricolour ribbon was so popular that it sold out before new supplies could be made. Street vendors carried Suffragette rubber dolls in their trays and offered "hever-lasting sooveeneers of the grite de-mon-steration!"

---

[1] Women's Social and Political Union

An enterprising firm presented Mrs. Drummond with accessories of military uniform especially designed for her as field marshal of the manoeuvre. She was to wear a peaked cap in the colours, an epaulette and a sash lettered General. This well-earned title was to remain with her throughout the movement and soon superseded her nicknames of "Bluebell" and "the Precocious Piglet."

The advertising campaign culminated in a "crusade fortnight" at the beginning of June. At Mrs. Lawrence's suggestion, bands of cyclists went out every evening on illuminated and decorated bicycles to distribute handbills and programmes in the suburbs. In variety theatres, the cinematograph advertisements invited people to the demonstration and featured short scenes from the Suffragette campaign, while every morning the women would be up early to chalk pavements and to distribute the mock tickets at main-line railway stations.

Three days before the demonstration, Mrs. Drummond hired a steam launch on the Thames. She drew up to the Terrace of the House of Commons and while brass band played, she unfurled a banner reading: "Women's Sunday - June 21 - CABINET MINISTERS SPECIALLY INVITED!" M.P.s, officials and amused servants came flocking out to the Terrace to hear Mrs. Drummond address them through a megaphone but she was unable to finish her speech, for very soon the river police appeared and her launch was chased back to land.

Mrs. Drummond was in complete charge of marshalling the processions. Thousands of women from all over the country were expected to arrive in London and a detailed schedule had been drawn up for their reception at the main-line stations. Stewards were on the platform to place the women in ranks as soon as they alighted from the trains, and once the processions were formed, each group of ten was directly superintended by a leader and a sub-leader.

June 21 was a brilliant summer day, and hundreds of Londoners came out early in the afternoon to watch the long processions making their way to the park with their brass bands and banners. Most of the women were dressed in white with trimmings of ribbon or flower sprays of violet and gardenia. Each marshal could be distinguished by her silken and gilded regalia stamped "Votes for Women," while the less important officials wore a lettered canvas regalia of purple, white and green. Groups of women from the provinces proudly carried the standards they had embroidered for the occasion and the largest banners, inscribed with long mottoes, were carried by men wearing huge rosettes. At every stage of the procession the women had the friendly co-operation of the police. Two thousand extra men had been recruited for the day, and their presence deterred any rowdy element from the processions.

Twenty wagons serving as platforms were spread out in a great circle over the park, and a pantechnicon stood in the middle of them as an information centre. From its roof, the "Conning Tower," Pethick-

Lawrence, reporters, and a changing group of V.I.P.s had an aerial view of the complete operation. Below them stretched a widening sea of summer hats, sombre bowlers, straw boaters, flimsy dresses, dark suits and light suits. As the crowd thickened, Pethick-Lawrence shouted instructions down to the police.

Already excited groups were gathering at the platforms and a gang of young men pushed round Number Eight where Christabel was to speak. when she arrived in academic dress, escorted by police, there was a general rush in the direction of her wagon. "We want Chrissie! We want Chrissie!" yelled the youths and they began to rock the platform.

"All togevva nah!" they shouted and roared out a popular song:

Put me upon an island where the girls are few,
Put me amongst the most ferocious lions in the Zoo,
You can put me upon a treadmill and I'll never fret,
But for pity's sake don't put me with a Suffering-gette.

Christabel impulsively decided to start her meeting before the arranged signal and as she spoke, her characteristic gesture — her outstretched arm — brought more people flocking to her platform. She walked round, addressing the crowd on all sides, and soon she threw off her cap and gown and stood simply in a plain holland dress.

For some time she managed to hold the audience with her quick repartee, but the bursts of pushing and fighting became increasingly violent. Children had to be lifted on to the platform for safety, and the mounted police rode through the crowd to loosen the press of people. No one could now hear what Christabel was saying but she continued speaking undeterred.

On the other platforms the younger Suffragette speakers met little opposition, but rowdies singled out Mrs. Pankhurst and Mrs. Martel who had so recently been mobbed at Newton Abbot. Mrs. Martel's wagon was almost overturned and two sailors, one on the other's shoulders, made constant interruptions at Mrs. Pankhurst's platform: when she mentioned married women, one of them bellowed, "Wives? Why, I've got four - all in different ports!" Then a bell rang and two men in the middle of the crowd started a wrestling match. People were pushed aside and squeezed together as the fighters made a space for themselves.

One of the features of the demonstration was to be a "Great Shout," called from every platform simultaneously at five o'clock. From the corners of the Conning Tower, four buglers announced the cry, and women with megaphones led the "Shout." "VOTES FOR WOMEN — VOTES FOR WOMEN — VOTES FOR WOMEN — ONE — TWO — THREE... " A confused roar came in response from the platforms near the Conning Tower, but further out the "Great Shout" was drowned in all the other excitement. At Christabel's platform the crowd cheered wildly, and as she drove off with a strong police escort, her enthusiastic audience chased after the van.

Supporters still remained in the park for hours afterwards. A country member wrote: "It was curious to emerge suddenly from an awful sneeze and a shouting mass of people to come immediately upon a little ring of fathers and mothers and children sitting quietly in the grass."

The Press was full of glowing accounts next morning. It was estimated that half a million people had come to the park, and these included a number of foreign sympathisers, and such well-known personalities as Thomas Hardy, H. G. Wells, Israel Zangwill, Lillah McCarthy and Bernard Shaw. Shaw's wife marched in the procession with Mrs. Pankhurst and he was a very prominent spectator. "I told my wife," he said, "that I'd go in the procession on one condition only — that I should sit in a Bath chair and that she should push it all the way! She didn't accept the offer!!" However Shaw raised his hat to his wife as she passed, and he remarked as he watched the rest of the demonstration: "Only one baby in the procession and that carried by a men; only one dog in the procession and that carried by a woman!"

Emma Goldman

Christian Evidence

Guy Aldred

"Orthodox unbelief and unbelieving orthodoxy!" - Moncure Conway

FROM 1904 to 1909, I spent a considerable portion of my time in Hyde Park, especially on Sundays and Bank holidays. When I first went there I was living at 133 Goswell Road, Clerkenwell, which deserves to be remembered as a very poverty-stricken yet really great centre of revolutionary activity and development. In January 1908 I moved to Shepherds Bush, where I lived first at 102 Thorpe Bank Road. At that time it was the end of the built-up area and from the window one looked across big fields to Acton. It was very much like living in the country yet with close access to the town. From there Rose Witcop and myself were compelled by economic conditions to "do a moonlight," but we only went a little nearer the Shepherds Bush Tube station, to 35 Stanlake Road. From here my so-called Indian Sedition activity was conducted.

After my imprisonment I went to live at 64 Minford Gardens, Shepherds Bush, which was on the opposite side of Uxbridge Road, parallel to it, and leading into Shepherds Bush Road. Here, the landlady developed a dislike to me and we moved to 17 Richmond Gardens. My activity as an agitator connected these places. Each became in turn the centre of an unbroken line of propaganda. The record will be retailed later. The story represents the light side of propaganda. Much of it is important.

After 1909, I broke with Hyde Park as a regular participant in its discussions. In later years, after I had established myself as a Glaswegian, I did engage in two Free Speech fights in Hyde Park. One I sought myself. The other was imposed on me by the police authorities. My regular consistent association with Hyde Park however, ended in 1909. In 1910 to 1919, it was casual. Mostly I had transferred my attention to Hammersmith and Ealing, but I visited Highbury Corner again sometimes.

It was my custom, during the period that I was almost an inhabitant of Hyde Park, to go into the Park for several hours on Saturday, Tuesday and Thursday evenings. Sunday, unless I was speaking elsewhere, meant almost a complete day in the Park.

I had made the acquaintance of Christian Evidence lecturers in Clerkenwell and Islington, in 1904, before I associated with them, or antagonised them in Hyde Park. Only, in Clerkenwell, they attacked me. In Hyde Park I did the attacking and I did it most vigorously. I also came into conflict with them in Brockwell Park, Regents Park, and Finsbury Park. During 1907, the Christian Evidence Society was at its peak as a reactionary propaganda association. After that, its influence declined. From 1904 to 1907 it was attaining to its height, Decline was inevitable because it had nothing to offer except blackguardism. It was an organisation without soul, without ideals, and without worth.

I was a keen admirer of Richard Carlile, whom the Freethinkers neglected, and Robert Taylor, the so-called Devil's Chaplain, in 1907. It often amazed me, when I was arguing with the Christian Evidence champions, to recall that the first Christian Evidence Society was established by Robert Taylor in London, on November 24th, 1824.

In the name of that organisation, Robert Taylor advanced four propositions which were certainly staggering issues for the apologists of the 1907 society to face. Robert Taylor, in the name of the C.E.S. challenged inquiry into the following points:

1. That the Scriptures of the New Testament were not written by the persons whose names they bear.
2. That they did not appear in the times to which they refer.
3. That the persons of whom they treat never existed.
4. That the events which they relate never happened.

Taylor advanced quite learned "proofs" in support of these propositions.

I certainly do not give unqualified support to these propositions, which anticipated the views and arguments of J. M. Robertson, Foote, and others. I think that they contain grave errors of thinking. But they were more reasonable than the unqualified superstition of the Christian Evidence Society of 1907, which was a reactionary Church of England organisation.

In Hyde Park, during this formative period of my life, I met many characters who influenced me. Some of them will be mentioned in this autobiography. The great feature of my Hyde Park activity was that I came into direct and untiring conflict with the Christian Evidence Society and developed a considerable contempt for the vulgar quality of this Society's dastardly propaganda. Its teaching was devoid of all spirituality. It was totally without reason or ethics.

My first experience of the actual propaganda of the Christian Evidence Society in Hyde Park was made on Sunday, December 13th, 1904. I then witnessed a typical example of the treatment which the Christians meted out to the Secularists in the discussion forum at Hyde Park — a treatment which was repeated constantly in my presence. Even in 1904 it seemed to have been but a repetition of similar treatment of mature expression.

As I was up there from about 4.30 to 8.30 p.m., I arrived in time to note that the fair-argument, free-speech-loving chairman, a somewhat old, and much bewhiskered gentleman by name of Allen, refused to allow any opposition at all.

At the evening meeting, Mr. McInnes, a fairly representative type of the orthodox buffoon, occupied the platform, and dealt with a book of Dumas. He touched largely, in the course of his remarks, upon the relative moral value of Christianity and Secularism. As I made notes, with the intention of offering opposition, I am able to give the gist of his lecture. Here it is:

"Christianity had given us hospitals, orphanages, and asylums. What had Atheists given us? Nothing but our prostitutes, drunkards and swindlers. Look at the 'great' National Secular Society! They had opened near a lunatic asylum, torn the Bible to pieces, got drunk on whisky, and removed to Newgate." He was speaking the truth; and before he left the Park that evening, he intended to defy the shoals of Atheists who surrounded the platform to do their worst. Atheists did not like to hear the truth, and therefore he suggested that they had better go and release their brothers at the zoo, the monkeys. As for Charles Bradlaugh, he was not worthy so much as to unloose the shoe latchet of the Quaker, Fox. And, where was Bradlaugh's monument? (Shouts — "At Northampton.") He stood corrected. So Bradlaugh did have a monument! Well, he was pleased that one had been erected to his memory. Although sufficient money had been raised to erect many more monuments, it was gratifying to know that all had not been dropped —

in beer, prostitution, and whisky.

Fox may have had his faults. The idea of this type of apologist pretending to have something in common with Fox the Quaker was nauseating.

Upon the conclusion of this admirable piece of humour, which had lasted for exactly one hour, Mr. Allen, the chairman, mounted the rostrum (which had been subscribed to by the public generally), asked for questions, and announced that no opposition would be allowed.

Messrs. Green, Bailey & Co, the general lecturers for the Society, which included a clean-shaved parson, owning to the sobriquet of Brownen, besides themselves, now arrived. The Secularists therefore, said brotherly-feeling Allen, would have to take their tonic from Mr. Green for thirty minutes.

The Secularists naturally raised their voices very powerfully and very rightly, against such lack of fair play, fear of honest discussion, and pious bigotry. Accordingly, Brother Bray, another Christian, went for two policemen. Secularists, unless they wished to face arrest, fine, and imprisonment, were forced to submit silently to this public insulting and dragging of their characters through the mire.

The worthy Green proceeded to administer his tonic. Here is an example, as offered without one bit of proof:

Atheism was unmanly, cowardly, brutish, immoral, beery, and not respectable; it was a barrier to scientific, intellectual and moral progress. From the asylum, the Secularists had gone to Newgate. So far as he could see, they were still not far removed from their ancestors, the monkeys.

Nor was this the most scandalous of the treatment meted out to the Secularists in the public forum by these Evidence quacks. Having removed with some other Freethinkers, while Green was speaking, to some distance from the meeting, I was surprised to find Mr. Bray advancing towards us and stopping dead within a few yards of where we were standing. The object was obvious; it was to invite banter. And while some was being indulged in, we observed the two policemen approaching, ready to "run us in" should we make a slip. Such was the freedom of speech enjoyed in the public forum in the year of grace 1904.

From 1905 to 1907, Freethought propaganda in Hyde Park was conducted mostly by the British Secular Society. Meeting announcenents of this organisation appeared in the *Agnostic Journal*. As all my *Agnostic Journal* were seized by the authorities, I cannot reproduce the names of the speakers and subjects meantime. Ernest Pack, who had a humourous style but spoke very distinct freethought, was the chief speaker. Another speaker was Frederick Howard. He was a born orator and a powerful propagandist. He became a Socialist and in disgust with Labourism, became an Anti-Parliamentarian. Despairing of the struggle, he became a speaker for the Anti-Socialist Union and was actually their most telling propagandist. When I knew him in 1907, he was a total abstainer. As an Anti-Socialist, he was not happy within himself, although he enjoyed himself making merry at the expense of the Labour politicians. He never compromised his Atheism. I met Howard often, even after I lived in Scotland. He became somewhat coarse but I retained my liking for him and regretted his associations. He was killed by a blitz during the Second World War.

In September 1907, Ernest Pack produced a curious two penny pamphlet, reporting a Christian Evidence lecture. The idea occurred to him of hiring a shorthand reporter to take down the address of a very polite and accomplished Christian Evidence lecturer, called Edward Baker. This report gave the gentlemen's speech as near as stenography could get to a phonograph; it reproduced grammar, pronunciation — and manners. This intensely interesting document was headed *God's Protectors* and was on sale at Pack's meetings in Finsbury Park. It is valuable evidence of what Christian Evidence lecturers were like at the beginning of the Twentieth Century. Baker was immortalised.

One great argument of the Christian Evidence Society in 1907 was to accuse the Secularists of having composed, printed, and circulated widely, a so-called "Whisky Hymn." The propaganda activity of the lecturers of this society made this hymn famous. At the time, Edith Fance was general secretary of the National Secular Society. She tried to bring the Christian Evidence Society to book. She asked the C.E.S. secretary to look into the matter. After much delay and evasion, he upheld the lecturers of his organisation and declared that it was published in a *Secularist Manual of Songs and Ceremonies* issued by Austin Holyoake and Charles Watts in 1871. The hymn was entitled "Let Us All Be Unhappy on Sunday" and only four lines of it were quoted. The Christian Evidence lecturers argued that these lines showed that Secularists advised people to sit at home and get drunk on Sundays.

Actually, the verses were not written nor published by the Secularists. They were published first in the columns of the highly respectable and orthodox *Blackwood's Magazine*. Later, they were included (pp. 120-122) in a volume published by William Blackwood and Sons, in 1879, entitled *Songs and Verses, Social and Scientific*, by an old Contributor to *Maga* — the author of them being really Lord Neaves. Charles Neaves (Lord) lived 1800-76. He was a famous Scottish Judge and a gifted song writer.

This volume was a collection of pieces that had been printed and circulated long before, and were brought together "in the hopes of preserving or reviving in the minds of those who were then pleased to approve of them a recollection of the feelings that attended their first reception."

The "Whisky Hymn" read as follows. Clearly this hymn was a satire on pious humbug and dreary Sabbatarians. The Christian Evidence apologists took two lines from it and said that Freethinkers preached getting "dismally drunk upon whisky!" Even if the hymn had urged this peculiar form of conduct, it was not composed nor published by Freethinkers. The assertion was a lie from start to finish.

Guy Aldred

LET US ALL BE UNHAPPY ON SUNDAY
A Lyric for Saturday Night
Air — We Bipeds Made Up of Frail Clay.

We zealots, made up of stiff clay,
The sour-looking children of sorrow,
While not over-jolly today,
Resolve to be wretched tomorrow.
We can't for a certainty tell
What mirth may molest us on Monday;
But, at least, to begin the week well,
Let us all be unhappy on Sunday.
That day, the calm season of rest,
Shall come to us freezing and frigid;
A gloom all our thoughts shall invest,
Such as Calvin would call over-rigid.
With sermons from morning to night,
we'll strive to be decent and dreary:
To preachers a praise and delight,
Who ne'er think that sermons can weary.
All tradesmen cry up their own wares;
In this they agree well together:
The Mason by stone and lime swears;
The Tanner is always for leather..
The Smith still for iron would go;
The Schoolmaster stands up for teaching;
And the Parson would have you to know,
There's nothing on earth like his preaching.
The face of kind Nature is fair;
But our system obscures its effulgence:
How sweet is a breath of fresh air!
But our rules don't allow the indulgence.
These gardens, their walks and green bowers,
might be free to the poor man for one day;
But no, the glad plants and gay flowers
Mustn't bloom or smell sweetly on Sunday.
What though a good precept we strain
Till hateful and hurtful we make it!
What though, in thus pulling the rein,
We may draw it so tight as to break it!
Abroad we forbid folks to roam,
For fear they get social or frisky;
But of course they can sit still at home,
And get dismally drunk upon whisky.
Then, though we can't certainly tell
How mirth may molest us on Monday;
At least, to begin the week well,
Let us all be unhappy on Sunday.

Personalities and Places

Bonar Thompson

A blow was struck at the livelihood of the freelance in 1926 by the appearance in Hyde Park of a large number of racing tipsters. These turf-guides attracted vast crowds. They were speaking on an important subject, of greater interest than any "ism" known to man—horse-racing. More people followed them outside the gate than had ever been known to follow any class of speaker since the Park was open for public recreation. Unfortunately the usual busybodies got to work, backed by a large body of lack of opinion. It was the contention of these prigs that the tipsters were a nuisance, that they lowered the standard of public discussion (the funniest statement ever made) and should be driven from the meeting-ground. The Calvinist communists and Nonconformist revolutionaries, together with all the Little Bethelites and professional spoil-sports, tin-horn redeemers and ardent humanitarian kill-joys, had their way as usual. An Amendment to the Hyde Park Regulations Act of 1872 was hurried through, and it was made illegal for any speaker to ask his listeners to follow him outside the gates for the payment of wages due to him for work done. This awful crime was called "Unlawfully soliciting donations," and is punishable by the imposition of a fine not exceeding five pounds.

This has made a considerable difference to the collections. I have used my brains and succeeded in devising a form of words by which I let the audience know that I could not be expected to work for nothing. This formula has served me fairly well since 1926, but I have been summoned and fined three times. The police have treated me with great consideration and allowed me considerable latitude, but no doubt they are compelled to take action occasionally. The rule forbidding the announcement of collections is vexatious and against public equity, but nobody cares about that. I do not myself. The only thing that concerns me is the loss of revenue which has resulted from the new regulation. But I do not complain; the fault is mine, for being a public speaker at all.

It must not be imagined that I thank those who cheer or contribute to the collection. They are paying for services rendered—that is all. I am entitled to whatever they give, and much more than I imagine any of them have ever thought of giving. I owe them nothing. The boot is on the other foot.

Three years ago I was approached by an official of the British Broadcasting Company and invited to speak to the listening millions from Savoy Hill. I was asked to avoid the subjects of sex and religion, but no other restrictions or conditions were imposed. The B.B.C. gave me a free hand to say what I liked. My talk was arranged for the third of May, 1930, and I was told by the director, as he handed me a very liberal fee, that my effort had been a great success. His opinion was confirmed by all sorts of people who wrote or spoke to me about it. It seemed that I had a good recording voice and a distinctive style of delivery, which gave general satisfaction. I was treated with extreme courtesy and liberality by the B.B.C. , and enjoyed the experience very much. I should like to speak in future to none but invisible audiences, and hope that it may some day be possible for me to do so.

By 1930 I was established in Hyde Park as the leading freelance speaker. I had gathered round me an audience which knew me and understood something of my attitude. These choice and master spirits would tolerate no interference of any kind with their right to listen to their favorite speaker. It was generally understood that I could do no wrong. Every one had to accept me as an orator unique among public speakers. I had no policy, no program, and no plan, no wish to uplift anybody, no concern for any social or political problem, and no message for humanity. I spoke on any subject, or no subject. Sometimes I put forward two mutually exclusive points of view in the same speech, and won general approval. I dominated the situation and did as I liked.

The large collections of former days could not be looked for. The depression had made a vast difference to every one. I did better financially than any other speaker, but there is no big money to be made in that way nowadays. My takings, on the average, during the last five or six years have ranged around the neighborhood of fifty shillings a week in the summer and thirty in the winter. Now and then I might have a record collection, but this would invariably be followed by a wet Sunday. I got engagements from time to time, to lecture or recite, but in view of my independent non-party attitude these became fewer and fewer. Whereas at one time I was in demand continually by Labour Party branches and other bodies, I seldom heard a word from any of them now. This pleased me very well. I had grown to look upon all movements as intolerably frowsy and silly. It was worth the money to be relieved from the awful boredom of lecturing to economic and political enthusiasts who were always yearning for a social system in which I was not interested. I was glad to be away from all that, never to associate again with the malcontents and puling protesters against everything which sane people take for granted. I would not lend my voice to the advocacy of socialism or any other "ism" for any sum of money.

When I look back upon my early career as a world-builder I sometimes wonder if I was entirely sane. The blindness, the stuffiness and stiffness, the fixity and rigidity of the people I cast my lot among, were incredible. Many of them have passed into their graves without ever having been more than half alive. It is fortunate that sane, humorous, and unpretentious humanity pays little attention to these agitators.

Normal people eat, sleep, laugh, make love, get drunk, get married, and get buried without bothering their head about holding "convictions," "principles," "ideals," or any of the big bow-wow humbug of the evangelist and the propagandist. That is why communism has petered out in this country. It cannot strike roots. The people remain essentially sane. Normal society rejects such fungi and normal humanity ignores them. The working-man prefers football and horse-racing. He may lose his temper at the former and his shirt at the latter, but at any rate he retains his sanity.

In the course of the nine years of continuous oratory in Hyde Park I have addressed millions of people. I have poured out treasures of wit and eloquence to an admiring and perspiring populace. My speeches must have given great pleasure to those millions. It has not been my primary intention to give pleasure to the masses, but if they have enjoyed my performances, then they stand in my debt.

One of my frequent listeners about this time was J. A. O'Rourke of the "Irish Players." O'Rourke is not so well known as Arthur Sinclair, Sara Allgood, or Maire O'Neil, but to me his stage-work is a source of unfailing joy. Within his range he is an actor of remarkable talent. As "Uncle Peter" in *The Plough and the Stars*, Sean O'Casey's great tragi-comedy of Dublin life and character, he is an unforgettable figure of frustrated self-importance and semi-senile goatishness. The lugubrious face, with its fixed expression of peevish determination, the labored rhythm of utterance, the clamping walk, the dreadful outbursts of sheepish wrath, and the gorgeous language of indignation and unctuous rectitude, which provoke derision from his companions—with what unholy accuracy and consummate skill does Mr. O'Rourke sustain this utterly delightful role.

I found Mr. O'Rourke to be a quiet, unassuming, unobtrusive soul; too modest, if anything, for he has great gifts.

I was once in Harry Hutchinson's dressing-room, having a talk about this and that with some of the wonderful players. Mr. Hutchinson, a fine actor, told a story of how, when he was once looking for a flat in London, the landlady asked him what his profession was. "I am one of the Irish Players," he said. "Oh," she exclaimed, "how nice! And what instrument do you play, may I ask?"

Sean O'Casey also listened to me occasionally. I first met him outside the gates of Hyde Park, where I had taken up my stand in order to collect my wages from the crowd who had been listening to me inside. "Hullo, Bonar; I want to have a talk with you afterwards," he said, and stood by while I took the few shillings I had earned. While he waited a man came up and said to me, "I wish I could speak like you, Mr. Thompson. How do you do it?" I get a lot of that sort of thing, and it makes me tired. It strikes me as about the most stupid remark any one could make. Exhausted with the intense nervous strain of speaking, I waved my hand and said, "A gift. A gift."

O'Casey broke in at once. "It's no gift at all. It's a matter of hard work and years of apprenticeship. What's the use of a gift if it is not cultivated and developed by hard work?" He took the bore off my hands and explained the thing to him in forcible language. He then took me home to dinner at his house in St. John's Wood. I have seldom spent such a profitable and enthralling evening. He talked of Yeats and Lady Gregory and Synge and the drama in such terms as showed him to be a man of intense thought and genius. I could have listened to him for ever. A kindly, sensitive, friendly man, with the stamp of great genius upon him. I felt honored to have met and spoken to him on such terms, and came away with the impression that he was the finest man I had ever met.

The rumors of his having lost his inspiration since he attained fame and success are rubbish. That sort of thing happens to second rate artists. Sean O'Casey is too hard-bitten, knows and has suffered too much, to develop swelled-head or to forget how to do good work. That his achievement is of the highest kind and will endure for all time I have no doubt whatever.

The only other man for whose genius I have the same respect (I have met a number of half-geniuses and have been told that I am one of these myself—God forbid!) is my great hero among actors, Mr. Ernest Milton. When *The Black Hat* was being started, I had a long interview with him and wrote about it in the first issue. I found him a brilliant conversationalist, cultured and witty. He is a man of great charm, a thinker and an artist of rare perception and great imagination. Everything about him is full of distinction. It struck me that this actor has something of Edgar Allan Poe in his temperament. There is the same suggestion of the demoniacal in his acting that made Irving's performances so memorable. Off-stage he seems remote, aloof, a sensitive and solitary soul. I have met him many times since then and found his conversation always attractive and delightful.

As a man and an artist, I admire him this side idolatry, a rare feeling for me to have about any of our modern celebrities, who have always struck me as commonplace and dim. It is a high privilege to be the contemporary of one who has brought to the stage such unique gifts of personality and artistic authority, who has added to the world's charm, and whose achievement reminds us that there is a realm of gold above the squalor of common existence.

In November of 1932 I was invited to address the Oxford University Liberal Debating Society at Oriel College. The meeting was a highly successful one. I laughed at Liberalism and attacked the most cherished beliefs of the students. They gave me an ovation at the close and treated me like a lord. One passage in my speech seemed to amuse them a great deal. "It must be borne in mind," I said, "that Mr. Ramsay MacDonald is not only a strong Labour man and an ardent socialist, but he is also a keen Liberal and a die-hard Conservative as well. His opposition to the late war was balanced by his active support of it, and while he takes a firm stand against one thing, he is equally firm in his support of its opposite. This is the secret of his rise to power."

This passing reflection, which struck me as so true as to be no more than a platitude, sent the audience into convulsions, and was reported in the Oxford press as a humorous remark. Every one appeared to be delighted with me, and I could not have wished for better treatment. The Society won general applause for their initiative and enterprise in bringing, for the first time in history, a real live Hyde Park orator to put his views before them. I was not, as a matter of fact, in the best of form for speaking, as I did not feel very well. Had I been at my best they would probably have appointed me as headmaster of the college, or something equally distinguished.

My health gave me a good deal of trouble about this time. I had to give up drinking any kind of intoxicants and go on a diet. I could not afford to take a rest or have a holiday, so I just carried on as usual. As I have always known how to use my voice, I did not suffer from hoarseness or any of the usual speakers' complaints; but my vitality was lowered, and this showed itself in my work. The speaker's difficulty is the heckler's opportunity, and I had one or two interrupters. I had no difficulty in dealing with them, but the fact that they had dared to open their mouths at all caused me to realize that I was losing grip a little. The crowds were, of course, secretly delighted to notice that I was in difficulties. The crowd is always the enemy of the individual, and only a fool takes notice of either popular hostility or popular applause. I brought myself back to full strength by dieting and deep-breathing, and regained once more the old ascendancy over crowds which has enabled me to avoid hard manual work for over a quarter of a century.

The Black Hat

Bonar Thompson

WHEN I am in good health I am in good speaking form, and I listen to my own speeches with keen interest and extreme pleasure. I have seldom listened to a speech of mine without learning something, and my platform performances have played an important part in my education. I should be guilty of ingratitude, worse, of discourtesy, if I allowed a meeting to disperse without moving a hearty vote of thanks to myself for what had been an artistic and intellectual experience of the greatest value. I generally lead the applause, and when I can afford it — which is never — I subscribe to the collection outside the gate. I only wish I could show my appreciation of myself in some substantial way, by an endowment or a handsome present of money, and if the time ever comes when material circumstances warrant such a gesture, you may rest assured I shall not forget what is, after all, an obligation and a duty towards one who has rendered for so many years of faithful service.

* * *

It was said by either Voltaire or Anatole France, or both, or neither, that to succeed in life it is not enough to be stupid, one must be well-mannered as well. That this is true in substance and in fact few intelligent persons will doubt, and fewer still will have the hardihood to deny. The tremendous pressure of stupidity, coupled with inertia, is responsible for all genuine success, especially in politics, the law, big business, and other forms of rascality and parasitism. In war, of course, not only stupidity but all manner of duplicity, lying, dying and such-like, is called for if. Either victory or defeat — which are roughly the same thing — is to be achieved.

CALLING ALL READERS

If readers of this miniature magazine are prepared to give me the necessary backing, I propose to establish *The Black Hat* as a monthly journal on a permanent basis. I launched the venture, as an expression of one man's attitude and outlook on life and the affairs of the world, in September of 1930. Without capital and hampered in all sorts of ways by circumstances of a peculiarly adverse nature, I have never allowed the paper to be used as a medium for propaganda or the preaching of any gospel. Articles from writers of distinction have appeared on rare occasions, but for the most part the entire contents of the paper have been written by myself. All the same, I shall introduce certain other writers to you from time to time, as occasion may warrant. Consistency, the hobgoblin of little minds, need not be looked for from me. Anything may be expected, or even nothing.

Barring accident I could easily live for another twenty years or so, if I could afford the money. But health, like happiness and long life, is a commodity that must be bought and paid for in cash. I would like this little paper to reach all my listeners but I'm afraid that is not possible just yet. If I had the money to do it, *The Black Hat* would be issued in hundreds of thousands, and copies would be on view on every bookstall and on sale at every newspaper shop throughout this kingdom. As things are I can only do what it possible for one man, and my health is not good enough to enable me to work as hard as I did in 1930. A staff is needed, offices, posters and the usual appurtenances of a publishing business. If readers will support me by sending their yearly subscriptions quickly, it will enable me to go on without fear of breaking down at the very start of the enterprise. If those in a position to send donations towards the Development Fund, will do so, I guarantee they will not be disappointed with the results.

After thirty-six years of Hyde Park oratory, during which I have entertained millions of people, made thousands of personal friends, and have not spared myself to provide good measure in entertainment of an unusual kind, I feel entitled to hope for support in this literary enterprise. It is a common experience for me to be told how my speeches have livened people up, cleared the cobwebs from their minds, and banished many of their anxieties and fears. While appreciating these tributes, I must say that while it is easy for people to say these nice things, it is often forgotten that my difficulties are at times very nearly unbearable. I am so placed that in trying to get paid for my work as a public entertainer of an individual kind, I have to go about it in a furtive manner because the Park regulations forbid the taking of collections. It is illegal to invite people outside the gate for the purpose of contributing money in return for services rendered. My payment is made up in such a way that I am driven to appear as a recipient of charity. It is altogether unjust and contrary to public equity. The hounding of Park speakers that went on at one time is too despicable to be written of in terms of restraint. But nothing is going to be done about it. I am sick and tired of speaking and writing about the penalties of Hyde Park oratory. The police are in no way to blame. Successive Governments turn a deaf ear to the legitimate complaints of citizens. My friend W. J. Brown, the Independent member for Rugby, did his best some years ago to get some sense out of His Majesty's First Commissioner of Works on this matter. Not even that brilliant man could break down the barrier of official obstinacy. My whole career has been made a burden because of this infamous regulation. My present state of health is largely due to the conditions in which I have been obliged to live and work.

I turn now to my readers and those who have expressed sympathy and admiration in public and in private. I need elbow-room in which to carry on my work. I have books and plays to write, and poems, articles and essays, and an autobiography of a new and quite original kind. I have lectures and speeches to deliver far better than any I have given in the past. I would like to present my single-handed dramatic performances in a small theatre, and propose to do so when my health is better — if it ever is better. So much to do, so little time to do it. It would be pleasant to accomplish these things and other projects I have in mind. It would not be unpleasing, I am vain enough to believe, to many thousands of those men and women whose goodwill I value very highly, if I were granted the opportunity of achieving these aims before my turn comes to bid the world good-night.

PEARLS OF CUT PRICE

It can be laid down as an axiom — I say it in all humility—that the man or woman who has never heard me speak has failed in life.

* * *

In my vegetable salad days, when I was green with envy, I had fits of priggish superiority when I became swell-headed through failure and was in danger of being spoiled by lack of success. I would pass a man in the street with my head in the air and refuse to recognize him because he had a lot of money in the bank. Bitter experience of prosperity, having had a bed to sleep in and two or even three meals a day, and the price of a seat in the gallery of the Holborn Empire, taught me that a wealthy man or a very rich woman may be a fellow-creature with a heart as hard as any pauper's and a handshake instead of a banknote for those in good standing or in bad. O beware, my friend, of snobbery! It is the green-eyed monster that will bring upon you the chastisement of *Hubris*, and may lead to your being thought better off than you actually are.

* * *

I have lived through three wars without ever feeling in the mood to win a halo of imperishable glory by laying down my life upon the stricken field. Many of you were too young to attend the Boer War, one of the best and cheapest we ever had, and well worth reviving, instead of launching the big and costly conflicts, of recent years. I was one of the first, if not *the* first, to forget to volunteer for that struggle in South Africa. I have never regretted it, and attribute my present existence and lack of solvency to that first step I neglected to take at the outset of a precarious and long-suffering career.

* * *

The vilest acts of which a man is capable have been done by good men for the loftiest reasons, and on principle. A man of principle, who is genuinely sincere and has the courage of his convictions will drench the world in blood and make the earth a wilderness rather than surrender his belief in some principle or other which he has borrowed from someone else, or been taught to accept, or acquired by "conversion," or some such nonsense.

* * *

Mr. Churchill makes speeches that read well, but he is not a great orator by the highest measurement. The greatest orator I ever heard was Tom Mann. He was matchless, unique, superb. We shall not look upon his like again. The great orators living to-day can be counted on one finger. More than that I am not prepared to say at this stage.

* * *

Every man has his price. Every price has its man. No act, however vile but someone will perform it if the payment is satisfactory. Horrible and cruel things are done for a very poor return too, like seal-fishing, for instance. The skins are torn from these friendly creatures while they are alive, and the men who do this are paid a living wage, sometimes hardly that.

* * *

When a monarch, a president, a premier or other national leader announces that he will fight to the death, he is generally in dead earnest. He is referring, of course, not to his own death — but yours.

* * *

Half the misery in the world is caused by ignorance. The other half is caused by knowledge.

* * *

Why should men work who have committed no crime?

* * *

No idea is worth dying for. It is important that this truth be realised, but it is even more important to realise that no idea is worth living for. All ideas come out of human heads; surely we know what human heads are made of by this time? When a man claims that an idea is true we should keep in mind the fact that we have only his word for it. If a thousand people, or ten thousand, or ten million people, insist that an idea is true, we have only their word for it. If all those people earnestly and passionately believed in the truth of the idea, and are ready to lay down their lives for it, this does not mean that the idea is true; it only means that they believe it to be true. What is believed is not evidence. And in any case evidence is only what satisfies a number of people. No amount of evidence proves anything except that a number of people accept it and are well satisfied that something is proved. In the long run they are found to have been mistaken; it establishes nothing of a definite or final description.

If physical courage could be eliminated from human nature we should all be better off. At the mention of danger all of us would take to our heels and remain alive and happy. We should keep clear of risk to life or limb and avoid dangerous work or any haphazard enterprise. But I must not indulge in Utopian dreams and visionary fancies. We are in a world of harsh reality, where courage, willingness to die in battle, and readiness to kill or be killed make countless thousands mourn. I would like to think men were capable of rising above such tomfoolery, such abominable stupidity, such odious orgies of death and ruination, but I am unable to believe they ever will. Call me pessimist, defeatist, escapist, what you will — I can see nothing in the future that has not happened in the past, and nothing in the past that is not happening in the present. To push past the present is like dancing with both feet in the air, or making a clock that will strike less than one.

* * *

Society is the enemy of every person in it. Every person in it is the enemy of society. Everything lives because something else dies. If you find justice, someone else has to lose it. You cannot exist as a living organism without injuring someone; bird, beast, insect, fish or human. Nor can you avoid doing harm to some life by hastening your own death. In the grave you will be a menace to the worms and a nuisance to many varieties of small life that never did you any harm. There's no way out: we are all assassins, parasites, villains. It is the will of nature, the great plan, the mighty scheme of things. And what a will! What a plan! What a scheme! A sadistic imbecile could have done better. He could not have done worse.

A GEM OF THE THIRD WATER

Why is Wordsworth's sonnet, *Upon Westminster Bridge*, almost universally accepted as one of the brightest gems of English literature? It opens awkwardly. "Earth has not anything... " is at least an ungraceful way of saying, "Earth has nothing... " In the third line the majesty of the sight presented by the City is described as *touching*. All the splendour, power and aloofness of majesty reduced to this little *touching*! Then, immediately the mind has pictured the City wearing the beauty of the morning like a garment, it has to perform an about-turn and conceive the ships, towers, etc., "bare... open unto the fields, and to the sky." And was there no way of getting the feet of the line right without that *unto*? Of Isis or Stratford's Avon "The river glideth at his own sweet will" might give an adequate picture. Of the Thames at Westminster — especially in 1802, when by all accounts it stank abominably — it is altogether too sylvan. Following that line we get, "Dear God! The very houses seem asleep." What is there about houses seeming asleep to demand that melodramatic "Dear God!"? And the "very" suggests there is something unprecedented and startling in an idea that must have occurred to the most prosaic of minds ever since towns were invented. Fortunately, almost as long ago as that, I christened Wordsworth the G. O. M. — Grandiose Old Man — of English poetry.

A JOURNALIST IN THE MAKING

To begin at the top in lowly failure and rise to success by declining steps seems a topsy-turvy mode of progression even in journalism, yet that has been my itinerary as far as writing is concerned.

I first burgeoned into print in 1922. It was obvious to me at the time that the existing social order was crumbling. A bold frontal attack by one of the master-spirits of the ages would topple it over. I delivered the blow in the form of five hundred copies of a pamphlet entitled *An Agitator of the Underworld*.

To-day a livid horror mantles over my mind at the thought of that epic work. A welter of alliteration leading up to a peroration of the clumsiest sentimentality, the whole printed on the cheap, soggy paper by two amateurs with a hand-printing press. I can only pray that time and its own demerits have consigned every copy to the oblivion of the incinerator.

The failure of the social order to topple at my assault left me blithely unperturbed and I immediately became a regular, signing contributor of eruptive verse and cyclonic articles to *The Worker*, a journal published in Glasgow. The immediacy and regularity are explained by the fact that *The Worker* could make no payment and had the greatest difficulty in obtaining any sort of copy. Pray silence for evermore upon all my contributions.

There followed a ruminative hiatus while creation no doubt gathered its resources within me until, in 1926, I siphoned once more into five thousand copies of a shilling booklet, *The Evangel of Unrest*.

Over the ensuing two or three years all but a few handfuls of these were sold and, no doubt, some are still extant in remote lumber rooms. I can only hope that no one will ever be so daring hardy as to assault me with the sight of one. Yet I have a lingering thought that there was, perhaps, some slight improvement on my earlier outpourings.

As I was always my own book trade and newspaper distributing association until *Hyde Park Orator* took the publishing barricades by storm, the sale of the five thousand occupied me for several years. It was not until late 1930 that I once more relapsed into composition. But the delay was worth the while. Apparently I was maturing in thought and outlook during the interval, for the next opus was *The Black Hat*.

The whole story of *The Black Hat* had not yet been told. In full detail it would be an epic comparable with the voyagings of Ulysses. Non-millionaire proprietor, editor, sub, advertising and circulation staff — I was all and more than all.

The capital involved was twenty-five pounds, largely borrowed or obtained from suits and a gold-shelled watch lodged at the pawnbroker's. There were nights of sitting with no money for fire or lighting, dashing off boisterous articles by candle-flicker. There were journeys devoid of bus fare to Tower Hill, Clapham, Putney or Finsbury, with a case load of copies for sale after an hour's speech. There were — but this is an article, not a volume.

Between 1930 and the present I have also made sporadic emergencies into orthodox journalism, but even these have been conducted in defiance of tradition and professional etiquette. I have not submitted articles, with two exceptions, in recent years. I have preferred to accept commissions offered by aspiring editors, and my photograph, looking out from beneath the black hat which had given my paper it's title, has featured many daily, evening and weekly papers and journals.

My autobiography, or rather one small part of my autobiography, *Hyde Park Orator*, entered the literary lists in 1934 and received a spacious and sympathetic press. With the rarest exceptions the Press has always shown itself generous and genial to me.

THE HORRORS OF READING

If one so looked up to as I have been for thirty-six years — by the audiences round my platform — needed introduction, I should announce myself as a mighty reader. I have devoted a lifetime of unremitting indolence to the pleasures and pains of print. For reading has its pains. There is the leaden ache of limb and mind that supervenes after five minutes of political science or one of the more vociferously lauded great philosophers. There are the sharper pangs that wring the withers of the soul in an hour with some newly pantheoned poet. There is the embarrassment of being faced with an author's soul laid bare and the realisation that a kipper is a thing of beauty and nobility by comparison. Yet for all the pains there are books enough that it has been worth living only to have read.

WORDS OF THE MOMENT

Nothing in those grim months before the war did more to sap my moral fibre than the word "escapism." It littered the newspapers and journals, echoed in the theatres, and ricocheted and reverberated through the clubs and coteries. If a convict under escort to the condemned cell no more than jumped through the window of an eighty-miles-an-hour express — not to mention if a bank-clerk read gangster stories or a shop-girl twopenny novelettes — it was escapism. Happily the war came. Or should it be unhappily? Now I am assailed on all sides by WISHFUL-THINKING.

THE END OF THE ROAD

My first appearance in Hyde Park was made on a warm afternoon during the second week of August, 1910. I tramped along Edgware Road towards the Marble Arch, passed through the gates of the Park to the speaking ground and began a speech right away. It was about three o'clock when I began speaking from the ground to a small knot of people. Although hungry and dusty after walking from Luton that morning, my voice was strong enough to bring around me a crowd which grew in numbers as I proceeded to lay down the law on the coming collapse of capitalism and the approaching world revolution. I spoke with vigour and vehemence, in an impassioned style which came easily to me. I expressed myself in language of fiery indignation of the sufferings of the poor and the needy, the oppressed and the down-trodden. I had the arrogance of ignorance and the staggering belief in my personal infallibility as a thinker and a critic which only youth and faulty education can produce. I spoke with feeling and sincerity on a subject I have made peculiarly my own, and upon which I am a leading authority.

I was broke to the wide when I began my address. When I finished speaking an hour later and went outside the gate to collect the financial returns I was a rich man. My financial assets stood at three shillings and fourpence. All said and done, friends, you may say what you like, but there can't be much wrong with a country where a young man, without influence of any kind and lacking the advantages of education and culture which are the prerogative of the so-called upper classes, is able to rise from the lowly sphere in which so many of our less fortunate fellow-beings are condemned to eke out their miserable lives on a pittance, and rise, by his own unaided efforts, from penury to poverty in the space of one short hour. I would like our young people, those juvenile delinquents who will be the slave-drivers and bomb-throwers of the glorious future, to take this message home with them and to ponder over it until they are black in the face. There is room at the top for those that get there, and glittering prizes in life's lottery for those that are able to grab them. It is by the exercise of those attributes which a just and prudent Creator has given to all, both high and low alike: thrift, punctuality, regularity, total abstinence, habitual continence, early rising, obedience to superiors and a devotion to what is right in the opinion of those best fitted to judge, readiness to serve, willingness to wait, a respectful hearing and an eagerness to listen to advice when offered by those set in authority over us, above all a habit of hard work — without which we are nothing — and a spirit of give rather than a greed to take, so that when danger threatens our costly homeland, and all we hold expensive is in peril, you will be proud and glad to fight, and above all to die, in the service of whatever Government may be in power at the time. Hold fast by these simple rules, accept with gratitude those sacred principles, and you will find that life has a meaning and a beauty of which we can but faintly dream, and a oneness and awareness of which only those that have experienced it can speak. You will find that piece of cod which passes all understanding, and that freedom which the world cannot give, but by and through which we are made the children of salvation and are counted among the blessed for evermore, both here and now, as it leaves me at present.

WHAT CRITICISM SAYS

Bonar Thompson, a world figure... was born in poverty... but poverty could not rob him of a rich inheritance of wit, melancholy, an artist's hands and hair, ironic humour, a love of language and a genius for making nothing pay. He mounts the platform, a slim, unsmiling figure with a poet's locks and a violent yet ironic revolutionary philosophy...

his character sketches of contemporary politicians were uncomfortably clever and many M.P.s and Ministers found their way to the stand to enjoy the pleasant entertainment of his wit. When the flying bombs came along, Mr. Thompson thought that this was the moment to take a theatre... he gave us Wilde's *Ballad of Reading Gaol* and caught the horror and the pity of it with a sensitive appreciation of his fellow Irishman's genius and personal tragedy.

> From Mr. Beverley Baxter's long and appreciative notice of my single-handed performance at the Gateway Theatre, Notting Hill.
> *Evening Standard*, July 26th, 1944.

Bonar Thompson is the pet of every connoisseur of open-air or indoor oratory. Time was when that witty, self-educated Ulsterman was broadcasting on and off, when he drank with visiting celebrities, and dropped periodical hints of his interminable masterpiece, his life story — which appeared at length with a preface by Sean O'Casey. I am glad I heard him in the wide-brimmed black hat he has all but immortalised in the spasmodic and ribald journal he used to sell after his meetings. A genius of open air. A fighter for democracy who grew cheerfully and resignedly sceptical.

> Stanley Harris in *The Tribune*, January 25th, 1946.

In a one-man show ranging from recitations of Shakespeare to a full-length speech in his best Marble Arch manner. He adroitly adapted his open-air technique to the dimensions of the little Gateway Theatre. He informed his audience that he had no party, no policy, no plan, no remedy, no message and no mission, and yet it was obvious that he was an industrious student of affairs and men. The message which one read into all his statement was that of tolerance. He added that he had won fame some years ago by being the only speaker who had not visited Russia. This is a pity, as Bonar Thompson possessed the grand manner of the Moscow Art Theatre, and in fact his reading of *Macbeth* recalled the style of some memorable Russian actors of the old school.

> *Manchester Guardian*, July, 1944.

I am by way of being one of Bonar Thompson's "fans." To me he represents a very healthy rebellion against the tyranny of slogans and catchwords, and a very healthy assertion of the individual spirit against the herd-like mass movements of modern times. It is a great pity that the individualist line which he is compelled to take, without which his very real genius would wither and die, deprives him of that collective support which he would be able to command were he to bury himself in an organisation or a movement. He should have the help and backing which his very rare and individual quality richly deserves.

W. J. Brown, M. P.

EDITORIAL

No MSS submitted for publication in *The Black Hat* will be considered unless accompanied by a substantial cheque towards the development of the paper. It must, however, be clearly understood that MSS will not necessarily be accepted because a cheque is enclosed. No work will be accepted unless it shows the writer to be a genius of the highest order.

* * *

Not every reader will enjoy all, some only parts, of *The Black Hat*, and some perhaps will be antagonized by it. No one will be, or ever has been, bored by it. Many have been stimulated and heartened by it in the past. Many readers coming to it for the first time have found it a corrective of sloppy thinking, sentimental hankering after the unattainable and impossible, narrowness of vision and the harbouring of ungenerous or cruel prejudices.

AGONY COLUMN

For over eighteen months I have not been able to write, phone or communicate in any way with anyone. I would like all my friends to know the reason for this apparent neglect. Until a few weeks ago, when though the unheard of generosity of a well-known friend whose name I will not publish at present, who came to the rescue at the eleventh hour, so to speak, to save me from a miserable descent into the ultimate silence, I was too ill to retain contact with anyone outside my place of abode. A ring on the telephone would go through me like a knife, and my wife had to answer such enquiries as were made from time to time. Four years ago I was seized by a painful illness which involved a long stay in hospital and three drastic operations before I was finally discharged. A long tour with Basil Langton's Travelling Repertory Theatre company followed, and by the time we returned from overseas in July, 1945, I had become so ill again that I had the disheartening experience of having to resign my part in *St. Joan* on account of this. Basil, Sir Lewis and Ann Casson,

Charles Straite, Douglas Campbell, Stanford Holme, Allan Judd, Joseph James and every member of the company treated me with kindness and consideration. I found it very distressing to be obliged to resign my part and leave the Company. I shall always retain friendly memories of happy times and of the personal stimulus and encouragement given me by Sir Lewis Casson. It was a pleasure to work with Basil Langton and Ann Casson, and, indeed, with every member of a distinguished band of players. Next month I hope to write about my experiences on tour. Meanwhile, I would like all friends to accept my regrets for my inability to communicate with them. I hope to make up for this very soon.

LECTURES

SEcretaries of lecture clubs, literary institutes and other societies wishing to avail themselves of my services as a lecturer should write me at 19 Arundel Gardens, W.11, phone Park 6869. The following subjects may prove of interest:

> The life and confessions of a Hyde Park orator.
> What Shakespeare means to me.
> The greatness and tragedy of Oscar Wilde.
> John Cowper Powys and the universe.
> Bernard Shaw on the gridiron.
> The blight of intellectuality.

The editor speaks in Hyde Park every Sunday at 2:30 and 5:30, weather and health permitting.

Bonar Thompson

Freedom of the Park

George Orwell
The Tribune, December 7th, 1945.

A few weeks ago, five people who were selling papers outside Hyde Park were arrested by the police for obstruction. When taken before the magistrates, they were all found guilty, four of them being bound over for six months and the other sentenced to forty shillings fine or a month's imprisonments. He preferred to serve his term.

The papers these people were selling were *Peace News*, *Forward* and *Freedom*, besides other kindred literature. *Peace News* is the organ of the Peace Pledge Union, *Freedom* (till recently called *War Commentary*) is that of the Anarchists; as for *Forward*, its politics defy definition, but at any rate it is violently Left. The magistrate, in passing sentence, stated that he was not influenced by the nature of the literature that was being sold; he was concerned merely with the fact of obstruction, and that this offence had technically been committed.

This raises several important points. To begin with, how does the law stand on the subject? As far as I can discover, selling newspapers in the street is technically an obstruction, at any rate if you fail to move when the police tell you to. So it would be legally possible for any policeman who felt like it to arrest any newsboy for selling the *Evening News*. Obviously this doesn't happen, so that the enforcement of the law depends on the discretion of the police.

And what makes the police decide to arrest one man rather than another? However it may be with the magistrate, I find it hard to believe that in this case the police were not influenced by political considerations. It is a bit too much of a coincidence that they should have picked on people selling just those papers.

If they had also arrested someone selling *Truth*, or the *Tablet*, or the *Spectator*, or even the *Church Times*, their impartiality would be easier to believe in.

The British police are not like the continental gendarmerie or Gestapo, but I do not think [sic] one maligns them in saying that, in the past, they have been unfriendly to Left-wing activities. They have generally shown a tendency to side with those whom they regarded as the defenders of private property. Till quite recently "red" and "illegal" were almost synonymous, and it was always the seller of, say the *Daily Worker*, never the seller of say, the *Daily Telegraph*, who was moved on and generally harassed. Apparently it can be the same, at any rate at moments, under a Labour Government.

A thing I would like to know — it is a thing we hear very little about — is what changes are made in the administrative personnel when there has been a change of government.. Does a police officer who has a vague notion that "Socialism" means something against the law carry on just the same when the government itself is Socialist?

When a Labour government takes over, I wonder what happens to Scotland Yard Special Branch? To Military Intelligence? We are not told, but such symptoms as there are do not suggest that any very extensive shuffling is going on.

However, the main point of this episode is that the sellers of newspapers and pamphlets should be interfered with at all. Which particular minority is singled out — whether Pacifists, Communists, Anarchists, Jehovah's Witness or the Legion of Christian Reformers who recently declared Hitler to be Jesus Christ — is a secondary matter. It is of symptomatic importance that these people should have been arrested at that particular spot. You are not allowed to sell literature inside Hyde Park, but for many years past it has been usual for the paper-sellers to station themselves outside the gates and distribute literature connected with the open air meetings a hundred yards away. Every kind of publication has been sold there without interference.

The degree of freedom of the press existing in this country is often over-rated. Technically there is great freedom, but the fact that most of the press is owned by a few people operates in much the same way as State censorship. On the other hand, freedom of speech is real. On a platform, or in certain recognised open air spaces like Hyde Park, you can say almost anything, and, what is perhaps more significant, no one is frightened to utter his true opinions in pubs, on the tops of busses, and so forth.

The point is that the relative freedom which we enjoy depends on public opinion. The law is no protection. Governments make laws, but whether they are carried out, and how the police behave, depends on the general temper in the country. If large numbers of people are interested in freedom of speech, there will be freedom of speech, even if the law forbids it; if public opinion is sluggish, inconvenient minorities will be persecuted, even if laws exist to protect them. The decline in the desire for individual liberty has not been so sharp as I would have predicted six years ago, when the war was starting, but still there has been a decline. The notion that certain opinions cannot safely be allowed a hearing is growing. It is given currency by intellectuals who confuse the issue by not distinguishing between democratic opposition and open rebellion, and it is reflected in our growing indifference to tyranny and injustice abroad. And even those who declare themselves to be in favour of freedom of opinion generally drop their claim when it is their own adversaries who are being prosecuted.

I am not suggesting that the arrest of five people for selling harmless newspapers is a major calamity. When you see what is happening in the world today, it hardly seems worth squealing about such a tiny incident.

All the same, it is not a good symptom that such things should happen when the war is well over, and I should feel happier if this and the long series of similar episodes that have preceded it, were capable of raising a genuine popular clamour, and not merely a mild flutter in sections of the minority press.

Freedom Defence Committee Bulletin (excerpt)

Freedom Defence Committee

THE agitation of the Freedom Defence Committee and other groups over the prosecution of Hyde Park literature sellers has had the result that, since the prosecution of Adolfo Caltabiano in December, mentioned in the last *Bulletin*, the sellers have been relatively unmolested, and no further prosecutions have been brought.

On the other hand, attempts to regularise this position, or to gain an investigation into the conduct of their evidence, have been unsuccessful. In January the matter was raised in the House of Commons by Michael Foot, but the Home Secretary replied that he was satisfied that there was no political discrimination, and refused categorically to hold any investigation into the rights of police action.

The Freedom Defence Committee then wrote to the Home Secretary in the following terms:

> In your answer you stated that you were satisfied that no political discrimination was involved. In that case, we would ask why it is that, although many thousands of newspaper sellers regularly ply their trade in the streets of London, the prosecutions for obstruction in recent months have been directed only against those who sell political sheets at Hyde Park?
>
> This Committee has interested itself in a number of the recent cases of Hyde Park literature sellers, and we have found that in all cases the police evidence differed from that of independent witnesses. In cases where it involved facts which could be checked, such as the width of pavements, we a satisfied ourselves of the inaccuracy of certain points of police evidence.
>
> As the police action at Hyde Park involves a grave infringement of civil liberties, we would ask if you are willing to see the representatives of this Committee, who will be able to present an account of the cases based on evidence in our hands, which differs materially from that presented by the police officers concerned.

The Home Office sent a wholly unsatisfactory reply:

> ... I am directed by the Secretary of State to say that police action for obstruction has not been confined to newspaper vendors outside the gates of Hyde Park and in fact during 1945 there were over two hundred prosecutions for obstruction in Oxford Street from Marble Arch to Oxford Circus. As regard the alleged inaccuracy of the police evidence, it is for the court to decide how much weight is to be attached to testimony on

either side. It would not be proper for the Secretary of State to discuss evidence in these particular cases with representatives of the committee, and he regrets that he is unable to accede to their request that he should do so. He would add that he can see no justification for the allegation that the police action in these cases "involves a grave infringement of civil liberties."

The Committee challenged this statement by asking how many of prosecutions for obstruction were directed against newspaper sellers, and by the following observations on the question of police:

With regard to the accuracy of police evidence in a particular case, we would agree that this is in the first instance the business of the court. We would, however, submit that the activities of the police in general are the business of the Home Office and you should be willing to hear evidence from both sides where complaints of police action are raised.

We would further point out that in one case during November the Marylebone magistrate ruled that obstruction need not be proved, and that use of the footpath for any purpose other than walking on it might be an offence. This is contrary to your own statement in the House of Commons, and we submit that merits investigation.

The Home Office replied with the admission that only nineteen cases out of two hundred had been those of newspaper vendors, and when the period and the number of daily newspaper sellers in Oxford Street is taken into account, the proportion to the number of Sunday sellers a Hyde Park who were prosecuted within a few weeks is very significant. On the question of police action, the Home Office again refused to agree to an investigation.

We emphasise the details of this incident to show the kind of police autonomy which is springing up at the present time, and which gives the police and the Home Office an attitude of defiance to public opinion or to the most elementary conceptions of justice, which is fraught with great danger for the future of civil liberties.

Personalities of Tower Hill

Donald Soper

PEOPLE ask: What is the good of Tower Hill or Hyde Park, or any other of the recognized open-air pitches? Is it really any more than an intellectual playground? I can very quickly answer for my self. After an education mainly derived from books, it has been for me an education infinitely more varied and valuable in the world of personality. Generalizations and labels must play a part in ordered thinking, and are indispensable to our logic, but their limitations are nowhere more manifest than in outdoor evangelism. One of the phrases I remember from the lectures of my college days was this: "The more complex, the less predictable." It is certainly true of people. I have long since given up the attempt to "sum people up" or to "know them through and through," or to "read them like a book." They simply don't fit into these convenient compartments like "The Man in the Street," "The Working Man," "The Public School Type," "The Proletarian," "The *Bourgeois*," "The Teddy Boy," or "The Square."

In the early days I spent a great deal of time arguing with a well-known personality of the Hill — tall, gaunt, bearded, with the bearing of a leader of men and the cynicism of an intractable disillusion, hostility, and defiance showing in every sentence of his oratory. His theme was scientific Socialism and his message cold and merciless. Not a vestige of colour illuminated his programme, nothing warm or winning punctuated his theories. In his philosophy economic facts and biological laws were everything; hopes and fears, tears and laughter were valueless. As he stalked the Hill breathing fire and slaughter against all religion, sneering at morality, despising the consolations of faith, I pictured him as a lonely man living by himself, despising the consolations of faith, disdaining the creature comforts, and nourished by the spleen and hatred of his creed. I heard one day that he had fallen from the wall on the Hill and was laid up with a broken leg. A friend of mine suggested that I might go and see him. Some days afterwards I called at his house. Unfortunately, he was out having his leg treated at the hospital, but I was able to talk to his wife, a smiling, gentle, and altogether charming little person. She told me that her husband was having a pretty bad time with his leg and was rather inclined to disregard the doctor's orders, but apart from that was getting along nicely. He was the best of husbands, but he *would* go about to all these political meetings! It was perfectly obvious that this hardened cynic of Tower Hill was an entirely different person in his home, and that in his own sitting-room he was by no means hardened and certainly far from cynical. I was able to leave them a little to tide them over their financial troubles. He wrote me a letter of thanks, shy, hesitant, and yet full of warm humanity which in public he derided. There are many tales and canards current upon the Hill about this man. I am not interested in them. In that brief episode the curtain was listed and all the complexity and variety of a human being revealed.

It is always worthwhile to know people. Therein is not only the true answer to materialism, but also the assurance of faith. Tower Hill has taught me that faith in human nature is not a barren, intellectual tenet. It is a living and creating force. The fact that I am ready to trust people, or that I believe that they are fundamentally spiritual beings, is not just a subjective fancy of mine, but an energy which flows through me, communicates itself to others, and alters things. Faith not only changes my attitude to my neighbour; it establishes and maintains a spiritual environment in which he is likewise affected.

Surely, to digress for a moment, this is the true answer to those who desire peace in the world today and yet are prevented from taking up an uncompromising attitude to violence because they feel that in certain circumstances violence is indispensable and reason inoperative. We do not live in a world which is static — the very problems we face are always fluid, and become manageable in the atmosphere of truth and goodness. To adopt a Christian attitude to a difficult case is not a forlorn hope. It is not a foregone conclusion that no matter how good you are the other fellow will always be bad. I am prepared to adopt the Christian attitude, not only to the reasonable opponent, but even to the lunatic or the drunk. I believe it works. I have often been asked after speaking about pacifism: Yes, but what would you do if an armed burglar came into your room — would you still be a pacifist? I am absolutely convinced that this particular and difficult case is the very one that is most susceptible to spiritual laws and influences, inasmuch as more than some others it has to do basically with human nature. I am quite satisfied in my own mind because, you see, I have had to face a couple of armed burglars, and therefore, without any conceit, I can claim to know what I am talking about. I was sitting in one of the small rooms at the Islington Central Hall, at which I had pastoral charge, one afternoon at about three o'clock. The door very gently opened and a tall, youngish man with a cap well down over his eyes poked his head in. He did not notice me, because I was seated right behind the door, and he whispered to a friend: "It's all clear; you stay there and keep a look out," and entered the room. At that point I made myself known to him and told him to sit down. Opening the door, I called to his confederate, and with a look of supreme innocence he also took a seat. I happened to know that they were both armed, and I am simply recording a fact when I say that they were in that state of mind in which in all good novels the burglar says: "It's a fair cop, Guv'nor." From my knowledge as a prison chaplain, I was able to tell them what the inside of a prison looked like, and I think, to show them something of the stupidity of their action. I did not turn them over to the police, but let them go after they had promised, for what it was worth, that they would try to go straight. On my thinking over this episode since, one thing stands out in my mind. How utterly foolish and futile would it have been for me to attempt the ordinarily accepted method of dealing with burglars! I do not know whether the man would have used his gun if I had tried to hit him with a book or "collar him low." I should think that is probably what he would have done. Superiority in numbers or strength was not on my side, but quite definitely I stood upon a moral ground which we all three recognized, and in the atmosphere of which violence was not only avoided, but superseded.

The point I am anxious to maintain and illustrate is that in all my experience of people the personality which is divided against itself is looking always to a unity in the moral and spiritual sphere, because only there is reconciliation and unity ultimately to be enjoyed.

Let me try to describe two or three of my open-air friends as examples. Here is a man. His age is between thirty-five and forty, his occupation that of a commercial traveller and his political creed a non-violent Marxism. He has travelled widely and read voraciously but uncritically. He is bewildered by the multitude of problems about which he reads, and still more by the practical difficulties and contradictions of the capitalism which he feels forced to serve. He is persuaded that the present system is all wrong and that Christianity, or for that matter any other religion, can offer no solution. He is really the most loquacious man I have ever come across, and spends his time at open-air meetings in quoting statistics and information from books he has just read or people he has just met, to prove what a mess the world is in. I personally know of nothing more irritating than to have to listen week by week to a man who has nothing constructive to say and whose outlook seems to be entirely taken up with the evils that surround him. He has reached that stage, probably familiar to you, of being so obsessed with the problems of life that there is no room in his mind for a faith in their solution. Many listening to him would regard him as a hopeless case. Do you mention John Wesley, then he has just read a book pointing out that that great reformer helped to raise militia and in family matters was probably indiscreet. Do you refer to the United Nations, then he has in his hand a pamphlet proving conclusively that the U. N. is in the hands of Jewish finance. Do you quote the Salvation Army, then he will produce statistics to demonstrate that its present General is a bulwark of Capitalism. Do you suggest finally that there are great souls who have overcome difficulties and changed conditions by the intensity of their faith and the creativeness of their actions, he will ridicule your assertions because he happens to know that behind the scenes all human actions are dictated by selfish desires and goodness is worthless. You will ask of such a man: Is it the slightest use to argue with him? I have often been asked: "Why do you bother with him? He is not sincere and does not want to know the truth." People who make such assertions are actually very wide of the mark. For this man is in an intellectual and moral prison from which, if he only knew it, he would give anything to escape. He has forced his way out once or twice. At the time when the question of the export of arms to the Far East was very much before the public eye, he said: "Why don't you do something about it? Why don't you go down to the docks and protest there?" I told him I would and suggested might come as well. He did. And as we walked together, I found I was talking to a different man. He was enthusiastic, humble and anxious, and although we could do little more than hold a meeting in conjunction with some more resisters who happened to be at the docks as well, he was as friendly and helpful as if he had been my ally for years. He escaped again from his prison after hearing that in connection with the West London Mission we had a clothes store to make second-hand clothing available at a nominal price to the very poor and, especially, to destitute ex-prisoners. He brought me some children's garments and asked me to find a specially deserving family to whom to give them, and he went away a happy man. He will never find the answer to his questions on Tower Hill. It is not the philosophy of Jesus or the theology of Christianity that will bring co-ordination and synthesis into his life. Like many others, a certain agnosticism will always find a place in his thoughts and views. Peace and satisfaction for him are bound up with activity. He belongs to the vast majority for whom truth is found only upon the march and conviction is "the wages of going on." During the last few months I have had the encouragement of seeing the beginning of that new unity. When I first met him he was entirely sceptical about peace. he saw the horrors of war, and yet regarded any attempt to escape war under the present system as a waste of time. Nothing seemed to give him greater satisfaction than to deride pacifism and sneer at disarmament. Notwithstanding, as week by week I have tried to impress upon him the uselessness of a merely negative attitude, he has slowly come to a practical decision. He told me the other day that although he could still see just as clearly the intellectual arguments against pacifism, yet he had decided to take the plunge. Instead of criticizing all Christian speakers, he assured me rather naively, he was going to give them his support. Yesterday, with a crusading zeal which is quite new he left my meeting in the middle in order to try to persuade another speaker to accept the creed to which at last he had given his assent. For the first time he may be making good use of those statistics which in the past have been his obsession and our despair.

Here is the real satisfaction of open-air preaching — to know that your witness for Christianity does enable you to help in this eternal problem of personality. To put it in the phraseology of the old hymn, to be made a "channel of blessing." This does not mean only that the speaker himself can be of assistance; it means that through him others, who want to help, are brought into touch with those who need them.

On many, many occasions a stranger has slipped money or a note into my hands with the words: "Give this to that poor fellow who was arguing with you, but don't let him know where it comes from."

A business-man of some standing gave me his card one Wednesday with these words: "I don't profess to be a good Christian but I agree entirely with what you say and I'd like to share in your work. If you come across a man on the Hill who is really down and out send him to me — I might be able to do something for him." I know of three men who have recovered, not only their economic position, but also their faith in Christianity because of that business-man's finding in me a channel for his goodness.

Of course, the big economic problems are outside the scope of one preacher or one crowd to solve, but it makes a world of difference when, instead of their being tackled from the commercial angle, two or three meet in friendship to face them. A new and creative atmosphere is breathed at once. Even if they are too difficult to be settled, they are invariably altered and take on a new hopefulness. Let me tell you of the Russian.

One day I was stopped in the City by a middle-aged man of intellectual appearance, carefully if shabbily dressed. He apologised for speaking, but said he had heard me on the Hill and would like to talk to me. He was a Russian engineer, a refugee from the U.S.S.R. His escape from behind the Iron Curtain had cost him his position, his friends and his money. With just a little salvaged from the general wreckage, he had come to England with his wife. He had obtained a number of temporary jobs, but now they had ceased, and he was at his wits' end. He asked me if he might send me his credentials, in case I should know of any vacancy, but much more than that he wanted to talk to me from time to time, as he felt the burden of his loneliness and poverty to be intolerable. I was amazed to find from his credentials that he had held very high and responsible positions in pre-war Russia, and was an accomplished linguist. He came to see me a number of times, and even though I failed to find him any permanent work I had the satisfaction of helping that man to keep his faith and his courage alive. He disappeared for some time, and later I got a letter from him in which he said this: "Happily, I am now acting as consultant engineer for a big firm. My wife and I are in good health and I think our troubles are passing. I am sure I should never have got through but for the spiritual fellowship I found week by week on Tower Hill. I used to come up every Wednesday to get the strength to carry on for the next week, and I was never disappointed."

To me, however, quite the most remarkable feature of the Hill is the astonishing way in which one after another hardened opponents of Christianity and bitter hecklers have revealed an expectancy with regard to the religion of Jesus, a sort of intuitive recognition that Christianity contains what they want, and have given me the opportunity to help them. It is true on the Hill as everywhere else — our critics do expect a high standard from us Christians. There is no higher compliment that atheists and Communists can pay than to turn to him in their real trouble. There is nothing which more manifestly proves the general assertion of this chapter: that religion helps where nothing else can.

One of the experiences which I treasure came to me in connection with just such an opponent. It happened at an open-air meeting I conducted near Highbury Corner every Monday evening. It is astonishing that, on looking back, I can recall hardly an opponent with whom in some way I have not been brought into fairly close contact. This man again seemed to take a positive delight in discrediting Christians and jeering at faith. He was always one to be reckoned with and on more than one occasion had the laugh on his side. As I was making my way along the Holloway Road to the corner one evening, he rushed up to me and thrust some papers into my hand. He was in great distress and looked haggard and ill. "Please read these" he said, "they will explain everything. I am in a terrible mess. I have just rushed away from a job I am doing. Here's my telephone number. Ring me up. For God's sake do something for me." I put the papers into my pocket, and after the meeting read them through and was able to piece together the story. This self-satisfied, cynical heckler had been happily married for some years to a wife whom he adored and around whom he had built his hope and his joys. Suddenly the world had crashed around him. It was a pitiful story; more than that I do not feel at liberty to say. I offered to go and see him, and sitting in his room I had the privilege of helping to put things right. Let me quote a bit of the conversation. He said: "I never realized that such troubles could come, but when they did I was utterly lost. I had nothing to hold on to, nothing to guide me; and I thought of you. I wondered if, after all I had said to you and about you, you would listen to me. Yet I felt that if anything could touch my problem it would be the sort of thing for which you stand." As he shook my hand when I left, he said: "I do not know how to repay you, but in future I will be the best heckler you have ever had." A few weeks later he was back at the meeting going for me with all his old assurance, interjecting, contradicting, just as he used to do. When I got down from my stand I said: "How's things?" He replied: "O.K."

Do men get converted on Tower Hill? you will ask. All that you have set down may be valuable, but, after all, you claim to preach Christ as the Saviour of Man. It may be helpful to discuss the merits or demerits of Christian institutions, the incidence of unemployment, the ethics of war or the theology of Julian Huxley, but do you get a verdict for Jesus Christ? It certainly is significant that the ministry of Tower Hill brings opportunities of personal service and awakens impulses to good, but what of the harvest of souls?

If we used the historic standards, I should have to confess that never have I seen a so-called dramatic conversion. Never has the meeting been interrupted by the spontaneous outburst of a man whose burden has suddenly rolled away. The conditions and atmosphere are patently dissimilar from those of an "evangelistic mission," such as is associated with indoor services or the Salvation Army. There is no opportunity after the meeting of following up the appeal — I am quite exhausted and most of the crowd have to get back to offices and warehouses. Yet conversions do happen. Many of them I hear of indirectly and long afterwards. It is the knowledge that the witness for Christ really does change the lives of some of those who listen that encourages me to go on, for, though one is not pleading for sympathy or pity, Tower Hill is always difficult and often dis]heartening work. I go, and I shall continue to go, because I have found Christ there and have been able to share that discovery with others. It is worth all the sore throats and frayed nerves to find in all sorts of unexpected places the evidence of the power of the gospel to save and keep those who hear and receive it gladly.

I was visiting prisoners in Pentonville Prison one Saturday after taking the weekly service for Nonconformists. I unlocked the door of C3 21. A rather pleasant and cultured-looking prisoner faced me.

I know your face, don't I?

"You ought to. Before I got this packet I used to be up on the Hill in your crowd most Wednesdays."

What are you in for?

"Picking pockets."

How many previous convictions?

"Nine."

This conversation was the beginning of many talks, and he admitted that the sort of religion that I was "dishing up" was new to him, and that he was thinking it over. I wanted him to promise to keep in touch with me after his release. He wouldn't do more than promise that I should see him sometimes in the crowd. Sure enough, a week or two after he came out of prison, there was the pickpocket standing deferentially where the crowd was thickest — a pickpocket's paradise — apparently absorbed in the debate. I felt a little apprehensive as to the safety of the watches in close proximity to him, but week by week passed and no watches disappeared; neither was he picked up as a "suspect." To my delight, he wrote to me some months afterwards from an address in the provinces to ask me to speak at a boys' club in connection with a Baptist church, where, having given his heart to God, he was now devoting his many talents to the services of the Master who had claimed him.

Of all the experiences of Tower Hill, the one I prize most and the one to which I turn most when I am inclined to be depressed is the following. I have been given permission to tell it in full and I do so with thankfulness.

One evening a young business-man came to see me. He was quite a stranger to me. With profound sorrow, he told me the reason for his visit. A little over a year previously, after attending the meeting on the Hill for some months, he had brought his fiancée to hear me speak. They were about to be married. He wanted to begin his married life in the atmosphere and spirit of the Christianity of which he had heard week by week. They were married shortly afterwards, and found together true love and companionship, in which they were gloriously happy. Later, as they looked forward to the coming of their baby, life seemed to them to be full. And then suddenly tragedy had overwhelmed them. In bringing that tiny child into the world his wife had given up her life, and for my friend the world seemed suddenly empty and meaningless. He asked me if I would conduct the funeral service. He felt sure it would be his wife's wish. It was certainly his own. I did so, and afterwards tried to comfort him. He wanted so badly to keep something of that faith in the love of God, and that truth that death is not the end, about which he had often heard me speak. I tried, foolishly enough, to argue with him, to present a case for the Fatherhood of God, to adduce evidence for the immortality of the soul. Argument was futile. Finally I did something which I ought to have had the faith to do at the very beginning. I told him simply, and without any attempt to explain or expound, the story of the Cross of Jesus. We spoke of His love and His sorrow, and as we sat together I saw his burden begin to lift. It was not as if the problems that were racking his mind had been solved, but that he knew that the awful loneliness had gone and there was One who understood and shared his agony. It has been a great experience to watch this brave fellow finding his way back to faith and to a certain measure of happiness. He said to me some time ago: "I never come to Tower Hill without hearing some word which I know is meant for me. It is more than a tonic. It just keeps me going." I see him but seldom. The last time we had a few minutes together he said: "I can honestly say that all that I have suffered seems worth while, for Christ has given me something to live for and something to make and share out of my tragedy." As I write this I can see the photograph of his little son on the mantel piece of my room. The little fellow's father is a fine and brave Christian gentleman who found Christ on Tower Hill and who, more than anyone else, has helped the speaker to believe that that discovery is one which all can make.

It would be impossible for me to set down what God has meant to me through this ministry. I should like to finish this chapter with a word about the friends He has brought me in this work, for the meeting is not only composed of those who quibble, those who doubt, and those who seek. I should not like to give the impression that the crowd is either mainly critical to Christianity or predominantly hostile. There is a splendid nucleus of Christians. I owe a debt of gratitude to those who have already given themselves to Jesus Christ and stand in the crowd on Wednesdays, not only to listen, but to support. They know that just by their presence they are helping to create an atmosphere. I know by their words of encouragement how they bear me up in their prayers week by week, are ready to defend me and to champion the cause for which we stand. Sometimes when I get back to my office the telephone rings and a stranger says: "You do not know who I am, but I was there on the Hill today. Do not be discouraged by the opposition. There are many like myself in the crowd who are trying to stand by you."

The crowd changes year by year: listeners come and go; but I think of four or five men who never fail to shake my hand and have a word with me before the meeting. I do not want to embarrass them, should they read this, but I should like them to know how much their friendship means to me and what a real job of work they are doing for the kingdom of God in maintaining that true fellowship which is His Church. There is the acquaintance of my school-days. The last thing I did for him at school was to give him a Prefect's whacking when I was Captain and he was a particularly obstreperous junior.

For five years, until his business took him elsewhere, he stood by me, times without number he made himself of service. There is the grizzled and lovable antique dealer who never fails with a word of cheer, and who comes with his wife from the other side of London every Sunday night to my church. There is the veteran of Tower Hill whose advice has on innumerable occasions helped me and whose personal kindness I cannot hope to repay. I do not forget my fellow-ministers, and one in particular, who, amid very busy lives, often come to the meeting, knowing full well from their own ministries what the stimulus and value merely of their presence in the crowd can mean to the speaker. And last, my severest critic and the saintliest man I ever knew, my father.

S. E. Parker, 1953

Lord Donald Soper

On the Platform

by Horatio

"A man who could have made his fortune in the halls."
— *Manchester Guardian* reporting a Party speaker at Trafalgar Square.

THE Socialist Party has always been renowned for its quite remarkable speakers. As a political Party wedded to the democratic idea, and "persuasion" of the soundness of its case, it was bound to produce a number of outstanding orators.

Side-by-side with its insistence on propagandist educational methods, went the refusal to countenance any sort of personality cult. The Party was what mattered; "leaders" were OUT. So here was the paradoxical position of, on the one hand, a number of quite exceptionally outstanding characters, while on the other personal grandeur had no place in the Party.

From 1904 onwards, until the great technical revolution, the "mass media" *was* the outdoor platform — or to use the Americanism, the "soap-box." In this, the Socialist Party was no different from the others claiming to be Socialist. The most notorious Labour politicians, in their day, were all soap-boxers. For years, many of them, George Lansbury (who was an ex-SDF paid propagandist), Jack Jones, Herbert Morrison, Tom Mann, John McLean, John Burns and scores of others, continued their regular street-corner meetings. It was the usual thing for any energetic young ILPer or member of the BSP to mount the street-corner platform. The main activity was the "meeting."

Despite its frequently much smaller membership the Socialist Party could and did, meet the pseudo-Socialists here on level terms. When all the public parks had three or four meetings running, the SPGB took its chance with the others, and the best man won — the biggest audience. In this school of fierce competition and deadly debate were trained some of the most brilliant exponents ever to hold audiences in sway.

The chief fascination of the public meeting was controversy. This it was which attracted thousands to all the local meeting spots. To hear Adolph Kohn, Alex Anderson, Moses Baritz, Charlie Lestor, Groves, Turner and others reduce Labourites, Leninists, Anarchists, Liberals, and religionists to stuttering impotence was sheer mirth provoking delight.

Since the Party definitely encouraged "heckling" and offered its platform to all opponents, victims were always forthcoming. It was the very success of the Party in demolishing opponents which instigated the decision by the Communist Party to forbid debates with the SPGB. No Party in this country suffered a more devastating attack from the SP than the CPGB.

They were easy meat. One recalls the packed meeting in St. George's Town Hall, Stepney. The entire East London CP there in force, our speaker Adolph Kohn. The local CP organiser requests a (loaded) question.

"Mr. Speaker, do you agree that all political parties are the expression of class interests?"

Kohn: "Yes!"

"Do you agree that separate political parties are the expression of the interests of sections of classes?"

Kohn: "Yes."

"In that case, Mr. Speaker, which section of the capitalist class does the Communist Party represent?"

Kohn: "*The Undertakers.*"

Collapse of CP!

Or Kohn's classic reply to the Hyde Park heckler shouting:

"Tell us when this 'ere Revolution is going to happen then?"

Kohn: "Next Tuesday afternoon at 2.30. Leave your address and we'll send you a post-card."

During the Second World War, events were relatively favourable to the Party. One platform alone stood in all its solitary glory in Hyde Park on September 3rd 1939 — the Socialist Party. The scene, and the impression it made, were described in an article in the magazine *Clubman* in 1955.

And from that day on, week in, week out, the Socialist Party doggedly held its ground against all the threats of assault and violence; against charges of "being in the pay of Hitler," "stabbing our boys in the back," etc. etc. As the war dragged on, the audiences grew. "I'm fighting for the likes of a little yellow bellied bastard like you," yells a fat uniformed Sergeant-Major on leave. "Then you have my permission to stop now," smiles Turner sweetly. Collapse of heckler.

Events dictated that eventually workers would leave other Parties and join the SP. Among them those who had been prominent in the CP. Week after week, fanatical Communists would shriek:

"YES! but have you *been* in *Russia*?!"

Speaker: "No! I haven't been in Australia either."

Heckler: "There you are then!"

Came the day when the same taunt was hurled at a new speaker who replied:

"YES! I lived in Moscow for many years as an official of the YCL."

Same Communist heckler: "What bloody difference does that make then?"

Who can forget the Conway Hall in London? The occasion, a debate between the SPGB and Mrs. (now Lady) Barbara Wootton. Packed to the doors — the record of that debate on "Federal Union" in pamphlet form speaks for itself. Or Shoreditch Town Hall packed, hanging on the chandeliers; Cliff Groves playing with Sir Waldron Smithers, who told Groves he would pray for him. Groves objected to him *preying* on him.

The Hammersmith Town Hall packed; SPGB versus the Peace Pledge Union. George Plume, Secretary of the PPU:

"It's all very well the SPGB saying that Pacifists are impotent. I'm the only pacifist in this country who got a month's solitary for striking a sergeant over the head with a chamber-pot." Or the post-war election campaigns where the opponents trembled at the thought of a Party speaker.

Traffic and television have changed all this. Politics has been plonked right inside the sitting room. A new generation has grown up in ignorance of the old heroic days. Phone-ins, quizzes, TV and radio have replaced the simple, direct, elemental, personal approach.

Who are we to deplore change — we are revolutionaries! Change is our business! Eventually we, too, will win our way to the media. One of the reasons for the high quality of our propaganda is the wise insistence that nobody shall speak publicly without satisfying the members that he knows — the speakers' test. A fault of our modern propaganda is the inability to answer questions concisely — like Kohn, with one word. The wit was devastating.

Despite traffic and television, public speaking will always be the Party's most valuable activity. Every member who masters it acquires a new dimension. The man (or woman) who knows, who speaks clearly and simply, will always attract and convince.

On our Seventieth Anniversary we salute the orators of the past, resolving to carry on their work until its aim is achieved.

Stop Speaking, I'm Interrupting!

Dusty Hughes

TEN years ago Heathcote Williams wrote a book called *The Speakers* about the orators at Speaker's Corner, in particular four great ones — MacGuinness, Webster, Axel Ney-Hoch and Van Dyn. A play based on the book opens at the ICA this week. What is it like at Speaker's Corner today?

A Scotsman in a black beret with a white goatee beard and a strong weather-beaten face stands up on his specially-built speaker's chair and a meeting quietly forms. At first there are only eight of us including his two cronies: a man in a trilby hat and a diminutive bloke with three teeth. Later there are a lot more including an even smaller Indian in a white mac who appears to be wearing a fez. On second glance it's a lady's hat, very like a fez but with lace round it.

The Scotsman's chair has a ledge that he leans on and under that there's a board with bold white capital letters on it. It says: "Robert Ogilvie." "It's not to tell you who I am, it's to tell *me* who I am." Ogilvie is the best speaker in the park today. He comes on like a mad anarchist Fyfe Robertson. But his meetings are small, more like brain trusts. "Now by way of starting the meeting has any body got any questions?" None, so he breaks into a tirade about the young, the uselessness of education, drugs, and manages to work in Milhench too. He works with a kind of sarcastic intelligence, drawing reactions from the crowd, developing the ideas quickly and with amazing clarity. When he grins his sardonic brown eyes wrinkle up. his theme is as broad as most of the other speakers' themes today are narrow; Life ... and Ogilvie.

"I'm seventy three. I stopped work at fourteen and a half and sent my mother out to provide for me ... Look at Rothschild, he never did any work. And look how far I've got without working!" Laughter. "I sometimes look at myself in the mirror and say, 'look how far you've got!'" More laughter. A tall freak with a black beard and a shiny top hat joins the back of the crowd. "Heil to the prophet Leary," says Ogilvie crossing himself solemnly. He ends the gesture with a V-sign to the freak who's advertising the Windsor Free Festival.

Across the way a black guy who is otherwise a pretty dull speaker is having his best moment. "The English are stupid. If you kick a Frenchman he kicks you back. If you kick a German he kicks you back. If you kick a Spaniard he kicks you back. If you kick an Englishman he's so busy saying he's sorry he forgets to kick you back. That's why the English are so stupid." An old one, but the crowd loves it.

Somebody asks Ogilvie what he thinks of the other speakers. "They're all exhibitionists. They're just unbuttoning their trousers and saying, 'This is my big prick, look at it.'"

"What are you then?"

"A narcissist," a big Australian shouts.

Ogilvie turns on him. "What are you doing here, then?"

"I came on the Piccadilly line," says the heckler.

"Ah yes," says Ogilvie, "the arsehole line."

The Australian, a bit embarrassed, shifts towards the back of the crowd. "I'm just passing through," he says.

"You better be careful on the Piccadilly line," says Ogilvie, "or somebody will pass through you." The Indian in the lady's hat, who smells of booze, starts heckling in an odd grating voice. "You dirty old man, ha ha. You talk fuckin' rubbish."

Fings ain't wot ...

Even ten years ago when the great MacGuinness was still alive, the "ex-speakers" and "speakers' critics" who stand in little knots on the fringes of the crowds were saying that the park wasn't what it used to be. They didn't know how lucky they were. There's very little talent about now. but even on a fairly chilly spring Sunday the crowds are heavy. The tourists have arrived at last for the season. And after all it is a tourist attraction. Sadly it rarely transcends that now.

MacGuinness died in Blackpool seven years ago of the speed and the booze. MacGuinness was a streaker before the word was even thought of — running stark naked through Regent's Park with a spear crying out that he was the last of the Mohicans.

And the most charismatic speaker of the lot, Axel Ney-Hoch, has given up. They say his wife has left him and his daughter's ill. Two days after Kennedy was assassinated, Axel was on his platform being jeered at while saying "The man who shot Kennedy did this because Kennedy was ultimately *unapproachable*! ... He was an opportunist, as is the man who follows him and the man who follows him. Assassination is an act of despair. It is sad. There is no alternative ...!" And Van Dyn doesn't speak any more.

Only Webster, who really is a star, is fully operational. But he makes enough money out of speaking to be able to winter in Australia, which is where he is. He only comes to the park in the summer, when the weather's warmer.

Webster comes on like Judy Garland, somebody says. He's spoken on every platform you care to name - for the Fascists, the IR, the Zionists, the Trotskyists, even the Salvation Army, finally ending up like the best speakers do, as an independent, a free thinker. He tends to see himself as the king of the speakers, and he probably is. While he's away he leaves behind a young protege — a Jewish boy who tells well-known Jewish jokes to a surprisingly large crowd. A few yards away a Zionist speaker is addressing a political meeting.

Most of the political and religious speakers are predictable: small organisations like the Socialist Party of G.B. (est. 1904), and some renegade Marxists preaching the gospel from the *bourgeois* individualism of a milk crate rather than the Home Sweet Home of any party. But one of them has the tallest platform in the park, with a red flag fluttering high above it. As a speaker, he's not exactly enthralling. But from a distance you realise he's studied every gesture and pose of Lenin from photographs. A long range performance; leaning forward or posing almost in profile, arms heroically up-stretched, or held out in obeisance to the crowd.

... they used to be.
Smith, known in *The Speakers* as the man with feathers in his hair, collects a small crowd. "Any questions, any questions?" he mumbles, hopping on one leg, looking wildly about. He breaks into a very bad version of "Chicago." A bearded sports-jacketed religious speaker is already creaming off parts of his crowd. Smith collects a few pennies in a rolled up, bashed-about newspaper. He breaks into his usual horse race routine, but it's mainly gibberish. "Apalachee on the rails. Apalachee is running in the two thousand Guineas soon. But he's odds on favourite, so it's not much of a tip. The crowd gets even smaller. Christine Keeler coming through on the stand side... Mandy Rice Davies on the rails, Profumo's making ground... it's Randy Rice-Davies, Christine Keeler's coming, coming through fast, Lord Astor's making ground... It's Randy Rice Davies, Christine Keeler, Profumo! It's a photo finish! What a dirty photo!" The crowd goes completely. He tries to get them back with Van Dyn's famous cry, "Aaaaahoooooh!" And again.

Van Dyn is leaning up against the railings showing his book of cuttings to a group of tourists and taking his cap off for photographs to show them the dragon tattooed across his bald skull. He's had three heart attacks and hasn't spoken in the park for three years. He just shows around the book with the cuttings that say he's the worst man in the World, and how he worked for Al Capone and how he was wrongfully imprisoned in 1931. Smith *The Speakers* does Van Dyn's cry again.

All the speakers are rip-off artists. Even MacGuinness used to tell some very old jokes. But the geniuses could carry it off, for the boy with the dirty jokes next to the Zionist platform they become the substance of his speaking because he hasn't got the experience to use the crowd. when somebody calls him a stupid git, he falls back on the old speaker's come back, "If I'm stupid you must be even more stupid for standing there listening to me." Worse still it could even have been a plant. Across the way Ogilvie has just physically ejected the small Indian in the lady's hat. That's very unusual. The crowd roar with delight. He hasn't stolen that from anybody.

After *The Speakers The Speakers* was published the speakers could be heard on their platforms saying that Heathcote Williams had ripped them off. But now it has almost become the bible of Speakers Corner. Van Dyn brings out a paperback copy to show me. It's got his face on the front. It wouldn't be too much of a surprise if some of the younger speakers start learning MacGuinness' speeches verbatim from the book, if they haven't done so already.

And looking around the park at the end of the afternoon, it wouldn't be too great a tragedy. We're all riddled with nostalgia anyway. Ogilvie is still going strong. And there's a dignified, furiously concentrating old man attacking groups of young ravers for their immorality and lack of spunk. But the dreary pink Divine Light van has arrived to scatter more confetti for the tourists and a group of pubescent Salvation Army lads are doing rhetoric training, stepping up and off their platform in a relay race.

Most of what everybody has to say is dull as ditchwater. The best speakers have always been the ones with the charisma, not the religious speakers, and not the political speakers anymore, who tend to get tied down within the tight confines of the message. Once you're in a crowd and you realise that you can hear what you're hearing in most pubs just before closing, then is the time to leave. As soon as this pub closes, as they say, the Revolution starts. But meanwhile there's a play about the old ones...

Joint Stock Theatre Group present

THE SPEAKERS

THE SPEAKERS is a play based on Heathcote Williams' highly praised book, a half documentary, half fictional account of the public utterances and private lives of some of the fascinating people who speak at Hyde Park Corner. Of the book V.S. Pritchett writes *"In THE SPEAKERS one gets a real inside look into London nightmare and London cunning"* and Maurice Richardson calls it *"fascinatingly original.......unusually vivid........ The combined effect is one of continuously present Apocalypse, most rare"*. This extraordinary book has been freely adapted for the stage.

HEATHCOTE WILLIAMS
Evening Standard Most Promising Dramatist of The Year Award 1970/71
Obie Award (New York off-Broadway) 1970/71
Arts Council's John Whiting Award 1971/72
George Devine Award 1972
These Awards were made to Heathcote Williams following the production of his play AC/DC at The Theatre Upstairs. His only other play, an earlier one, is The Local Stigmatic which has been revived on a number of occasions since its premiere at the Traverse, Edinburgh in 1967. Although these are the only two plays he has written, they have established Heathcote Williams' reputation as a quite remarkable and unusual playwright.

WILLIAM GASKILL
Associate Director of The National Theatre 1963/65
Artistic Director of the English Stage Company 1965/72.

His many productions include Richard III, The Caucasian Chalk Circle, Cymbeline (all for the Royal Shakespeare Company); The Recruiting Officer, Philoctetes, The Dutch Courtesan, Mother Courage, Armstrong's Last Goodnight, The Beaux Stratagem (all for the National Theatre); Epitaph for George Dillon, Saved, Macbeth, The Three Sisters, Man is Man, Lear (by E. Bond) Big Wolf and many others at the Royal Court and elsewhere.

MAX STAFFORD-CLARK
Artistic Director of the Traverse Theatre 1968/72
Subsequently ran the Traverse Workshop Company for three years and directed Our Sunday Times, In The Heart of the British Museum, and Hitler Dances; also directed Slag by David Hare and Magnificence by Howard Brenton at the Royal Court where he was a resident Director.

JOINT STOCK THEATRE GROUP is a Company formed in London by David Aukin, David Hare and Max Stafford-Clark to provide an out-let for new work. It intends to act as an umbrella company for different projects.
THE SPEAKERS is Joint Stock's first production and it will be followed by a new play by Stanley Eveling.

The actors
Oliver Cotton
Paul Freeman
Roderic Leigh
Roger Lloyd Pack
Struan Rodgers
Tony Rohr
Toby Salaman
Jennie Stoller

Stage Manager
Ross Murray

Designer
Miki van Zwanenberg

Producer
David Aukin

a free adaptation of the book
by **Heathcote Williams**

Directed by
William Gaskill & Max Stafford-Clark

TERRACE THEATRE (ICA), Nash House, The Mall, SW1

JOINT STOCK THEATRE GROUP present

"THE SPEAKERS"

based on the book by HEATHCOTE WILLIAMS
freely adapted by William Gaskill and
Max Stafford-Clark

The action takes place in London, 1963.

Cast:
Oliver Cotton	Axel Ney Hoch
Ken Cranham	Cafferty
Paul Freeman	Jacobus Van Dyn
Cecily Hobbs	Freddie Kilennen, Gladys, Betty Dracup, Singing Woman, Rowton House Clerk.
Roderic Leigh	Socialist Speaker, Norman, Newsvendor, Colin, Bolling, N.A.B. Officer, Mary Pickford, Policeman.
Roger Lloyd Pack	Harry, Policeman, Doctor, Davies Prison Warder, Dealer.
Tony Rohr	William MacGuinness
Toby Salaman	Lomas

directed by WILLIAM GASKILL and MAX STAFFORD-CLARK

designer: Miki van Zwanenberg
stage manager: Ross Murray
photographs: John Haynes

lighting devised by White Light
lighting operator: Peter Hunt
wig: Kenneth Lintott

manager: David Aukin

For the ICA
General Manager   Joe Aveline
Operations Manager   Nigel Frith
Administration   Katherine Bint
Press   Susan Cussins (930 0493)

The play, "The Speakers", based on Heathcote Williams' book of the same title was produced at the ICA. 30th April – 18th May 1974 by the Joint Stock Theatre Group.

Irving Wardle in the Times
"London's most celebrated street theatre has been brought indoors... brilliant."

Eric Shorter in the Daily Telegraph
"The acting is always admirable."

Keith Dewhurst in the Guardian
"One rarely sees work of such intensity at such point-blank range, and this could lead to extraordinary moments."

John Peter in the Sunday Times
"A picture, savagely realistic and a little nostalgic, of a vanishing way of life and a breed of urban nomads."

for a LIMITED RUN at the
TERRACE THEATRE, ICA
Nash House, The Mall, SW1. Box Office: 930 6393
Tuesday 30th April to Saturday 18th May.
Tues – Thurs. 8 pm. Fri & Sat 7 pm and 9.15 pm.

Triumph of the Stage Irishman

The Guardian

Our Dublin Correspondent on the night an audience exceeded its role.

THE Abbey Theatre in Dublin, whose first experience of audience participation came unstuck at the weekend, will not be put off similar experiments in future. But its artistic director, Mr Tomas MacAnna, admitted yesterday that they would have to take greater care over who was admitted to the audience.

The disruption brought the Dublin Theatre Festival alive in its eleventh hour on Friday night with a hallowed tradition of the Irish stage. Two policemen stood menacingly by the Abbey's stage as the audience mingled with actors who had abandoned their planned performance. But, unlike the celebrated "Abbey riots" of the 1920s, the play was not halted by audience protests. Instead, the actors and management abandoned it after they had proved unable to cope with the audience.

The Joint Stock Company from London was staging its production of *The Speakers*, hailed by critics as a highly successful experiment in participatory drama. But it collapsed for the first time ever when some members of the audience refused to observe the rules of the game.

Mr. MacAnna accused those involved of deliberately attempting to disrupt the show. But he felt that it had been a worth-while experience. "The majority view of the audiences was that it was a most interesting and original and challenging experience."

The play, based on a book by Heathcote Williams, tries to recreate Speakers' Corner in Hyde Park in 1964. The audience shares the stage with the cast. They are invited to participate in the scenes depicting the speakers' public performances but not when the actors sketch out the orators' private lives.

Among the audience at the Abbey's late-night show on Friday was the Irish Republic's President, Mr Ó Dálaigh, an avid theatre goer. But he had left, as planned, shortly before the performance was abandoned.

The actors' difficulties began with one man who constantly heckled the speakers with obscene suggestions. Their tactics for dealing with hecklers contained him for a while but he kept up a constant barrage of four-letter words. At one stage he physically attacked an actor dressed as a London policeman, yelling "Pig, pig," after the "policeman" had attempted to arrest an Irish speaker.

The heckler's activities gradually dissolved the atmosphere of audience cooperation. Some verbally attacked him, while others voiced discontent with the play. It came to a head when two real policemen appeared at the side of the stage as theatre staff tried to edge the heckler and has companions out. But others in the audience objected. They suggested that the group had got the participation they had asked for and could scarcely complain if they got too much. One man commented angrily: "You set up the situation to manipulate us."

The planned performance disintegrated as attention switched to the new dramatic centre. The heckler said plaintively that he was only behaving as he always did in Hyde Park. One of the speakers portrayed by the cast had been a pal of his, he said.

The confusion grew as politics became involved. The heckler accused the two "real" policemen of being the killers of a Provisional IRA man shot dead in prison last year. Somehow the IRA hunger striker, Frank Stagg, was dragged into it along with Noel and Marie Murray, the couple awaiting execution for the murder of a policeman.

"The same people who subsidise this theatre are going to hang two people next month," the heckler announced from a ladder used earlier by one of the re-created speakers.

The actors eventually withdrew and half the audience left, including the heckler and his friends. Later the actors returned and a post mortem began. One of the cast commented that the man had intended to make a political point and had simply done so. He was drunk, an Abbey man proclaimed, just a rowdy.

With actors, audience, and management now on an equal footing someone inevitably suggested that they discuss the experience. Whither participatory theatre? and so forth.

A disillusioned drama-lover conmented in disgust: "Go back to proscenium theatre." An elderly woman suggested that the hecklers had "minds like sewers." And the Abbey's manager, Mr David Liddy, commented sadly: "This is our first show of this nature and probably the last."

But it was not. Joint Stock completed their programme with two more performances on Saturday. Participation remained within acceptable — and respectable — limits and the company left Dublin yesterday to perform at Cheltenham last night.

Park Regulations

HMSO

Park Regulation Act, 27th June, 1872
An Act for the Regulation of the Royal Parks and Gardens

WHEREAS it is expedient to protect from injury the Royal parks, gardens, and possessions under the management of the Commissioners of Her Majesty's Works and Public Buildings, hereinafter called the Commissioners, and to secure the public from molestation and annoyance while enjoying such parks, gardens, and possessions:

And whereas a list of such of the said parks and gardens and possessions as are now under the management of the Commissioners is contained in the Second Schedule hereto: Be it enacted by the Queen's Most Excellent Majesty, by and with the advice and consent of the Lords Spiritual and Temporal, and Commons, in this present Parliament assembled, and by the authority of the same, as follows:

Short Title
1. This Act may be cited for all purposes as "The Parks Regulation Act, 1872."

Application of Act.
2. (Repealed by 16 & 17 Geo. 5, Ch. 36.)

Definition of "Park Keeper."
3. "Park-keeper" shall mean any person who, previously to the passing of this Act, has been or may hereafter be appointed keeper of a park as defined by this Act.

Penalty on Violating Regulations in Schedule.
4. (Repealed by 16 & 17 Geo. 5, Ch. 36.)

Park-Keeper May Apprehend Any Offender Whose Name or Residence is Not Known.
5. Any park-keeper in uniform, and any persons whom he may call to his assistance, may take into custody, without a warrant, any offender who in the park where such keeper has jurisdiction, and within the view of such keeper, acts in contravention of any of the said regulations, provided that the name or residence of such offender is unknown to and cannot be ascertained by such park-keeper. If any such offender, when required by any park keeper or by any police constable to give his name and address, gives a false name or false address, he shall, on conviction by a court of summary jurisdiction, be liable to a penalty not exceeding five pounds.

Penalty on Assaults on Park-Keeper.
6. Where any person is convicted of an assault on any park-keeper when in the execution of his duty, such person shall, on conviction by a court of summary jurisdiction, in the discretion of the court, be liable either to pay a penalty not exceeding twenty pounds, and in default of payment to be imprisoned, with or without hard labour, for a tern not exceeding six months, or to be imprisoned for any term not exceeding six months, with or without hard labour.

Powers, Duties, and Privileges of Park-Keeper.
7. Every park-keeper, in addition to any powers and immunities specially conferred on him by this Act, shall, within the limits of the park of which he is keeper, have all such powers, privileges, and inmunities, and be liable to all such duties and responsibilities, as any police constable has within the police district in which such park is situated; and any person so appointed a park-keeper as aforesaid shall obey such lawful commands as he may from time to time receive from the Commissioners in respect of his conduct in the execution of his office.

Police Constables to Have the Same Powers, &c., as Park-Keepers.
8. Every police constable belonging to the police force of the district in which any park to which this Act applies is situate shall have the powers, privileges, and immunities of a park-keeper within such a park.

Rules to be Laid Before Parliament.
9. (Repealed by 16 & 17 Geo. 5, Ch. 36.)

Publication of Regulations.
10. Copies of regulations to be observed in pursuance of this Act by persons using a park to which this Act applies shall be put up in such park in such conspicuous manner as the Commissioners may deem best calculated to give information to the persons using the park.

Saving of Certain Rights.
11. Nothing in this Act shall authorise any interference with any rights of way or any right whatever to which any person or persons may be by law entitled.

Act to Be Cumulative.
12. All powers conferred by this Act shall be deemed to be in addition to and not in derogation of any powers conferred by any other Act of Parliament, and any such powers may be exercised as if this Act had not been passed.

Saving of the Rights of the Crown.
13. Nothing in this Act contained shall be deemed to prejudice or affect any prerogative or right of Her Majesty, or any power, right, or duty of the Commissioners, or any powers, or duties of any officers, clerks, or servants, appointed by Her Majesty or by the Commissioners.

Saving of Metropolitan Streets Act.
14. Nothing in this Act contained shall affect the metropolitan Streets Act, 1867, or the application thereof to any park to which it is by law applicable.

Summary Proceedings for Offences.
15. Any offence against this Act may be prosecuted before a court of summary jurisdiction as follows:

In England, in manner directed by the Act of the session of the eleventh and twelfth years of the reign of Her present Majesty, chapter forty-three, entitled "An Act to facilitate the performance of the duties of justices of the peace out of sessions within England and Wales with respect to summary convictions and orders," and any Act amending the last-mentioned Act.

In Scotland, the court of summary jurisdiction shall include any justice or justices of the peace, sheriff or sheriff substitute, police or other magistrate, proceedings before whom may be regulated by "The Summary Procedure Act, 1864," upon whom all jurisdictions, powers, and authorities necessary for the purposes of this Act are hereby conferred.

All offences under this Act in Scotland shall be prosecuted and all penalties recovered under the provisions of the Summary Procedure Act, 1864, at the instance of the procurator fiscal of the court before which such proceedings are instituted.

In Scotland, all penalties under this Act, other than those hereinbefore provided for, in default of payment may be enforced by imprisonment for a term to be specified in the judgement or sentence of the court, but not exceeding three calendar months; and all penalties imposed and recovered under this Act shall be paid to the clerk of court, and by him accounted for and paid to the fine fund of the court in which the fine is imposed.

"Court of summary jurisdiction" shall in this Act mean and include any justice or justices of the peace, metropolitan police magistrate, stipendiary or other magistrate or officer, by whatever name called, to whom jurisdiction in respect of offences arising under this Act is given by this section or any Acts therein referred to.

NOTE. The two Schedules to this Act were repealed by 16 & 17 Geo. 5, Ch. 36.

Statutory Instruments
1955 No. 1750; Open Spaces
The Hyde Park Regulations, 1955

Draft Laid Before Parliament	14th July, 1955
Made	22nd November, 1955
Coming into Operation	6th December, 1955

THE minister of Works, in exercise of the powers conferred upon him by the Parks Regulation Acts, 1872[1] and 1926[2], and of all other powers enabling him in that behalf, hereby makes the following Regulations:

I. Interpretation

1. In these Regulations: "the Minister" means the Minister of Works; "the park" means Hyde Park; "the bathing area" means the area in the Serpentine for the time being marked by buoys as reserved for bathing; "the riding ways" means the roads for the time being open to vehicular traffic and the horse rides known as Rotten Row, the North Ride and the New Ride; "the public speaking area" means the area enclosed by the North Side running from the Marble Arch to the Victoria Gate and thence to the magazine along the Serpentine to Hyde Park Corner and the Broad walk running from Hyde Park Corner to the Marble Arch and including the footway at the junction of the North and East Carriage Drives known as Speakers' Corner.

2. The Interpretation Act, 1889[3] shall apply to these Regulations as it applies to an Act of Parliament.

3. These Regulations may be cited as The Hyde Park Regulations, 1955.

II. Prohibited Acts

Within the Park the following acts are prohibited:

1. failing to conform to any directions for the regulation of traffic given by a Park-Keeper or Police Constable or by a notice or sign exhibited by order of the Minister;

2. driving or riding at a speed greater than twenty miles an hour[4];

3. failing to remove a vehicle after having been requested to do so by a Park Keeper or Police Constable;

4. soliciting passengers with a hackney carriage;

5. failing to keep any animal under control, or on a lead where required by notice to do so;

6. permitting any animal to be in the bathing area or in any boat;

---

[1] 35 & 36 Vict. c. 15.
[2] 16 & 17 Geo. 5 c. 36.
[3] 52 & 53 Vict. c. 63.
[4] The figure of twenty miles an hour is amended to thirty miles an hour by the Hyde Park (First Amendment) Regulations. 1960, S.I. 1960, NO. 1233.

7. failure by any person having charge of any animal to remove it from the Park on being requested by a Park-Keeper or Police Constable to do so;

8. failing to conform to any directions for the regulation of horses or riding given by a Park Keeper or Police Constable or by a notice or sign exhibited by order of the Minister;

9. riding in any manner likely to cause danger or inconvenience to persons in the Park, including other riders;

10. wilfully disturbing or injuring any animal, fish, or bird, or taking any egg;

11. entering any part of the Park after having been requested by a Park Keeper or Police Constable not to do so;

12. remaining in any part of the Park after having been requested by a Park keeper or Police Constable to leave it;

13. wilfully interfering with the comfort or convenience of any person in the Park;

14. collecting or soliciting money;

15. dropping or leaving litter except in a receptacle provided for the purpose;

16. any act which pollutes or is likely to pollute any water;

17. climbing trees or railings, fences or structures of any other kind;

18. playing any game or engaging in any form of sport or exercise after being requested by a Park-Keeper or Police Constable not to do so;

19. using any mechanically propelled or operated model after having been requested by a Park-Keeper or Police Constable not to do so;

20. sailing model boats;

21. behaving or being clothed in any manner reasonably likely to offend against public decency;

22. bathing except within the bathing area;

23. boating (a) in the bathing area or in an area enclosed for any purpose, or (b) except at a time when boating is permitted by notice or sign exhibited by order of the Minister;

24. embarking in or disembarking from a boat elsewhere than at a place appointed by the Minister for that purpose;

25. breaking or damaging any ice, throwing things upon it, or any other act in relation to it which is likely to interfere with the safety or convenience of skaters;

26. obstructing, or otherwise interfering with free passage on, any road or path;

27. obstructing or interfering with any parade, review, procession or assembly authorised by the Minister;

28. behaviour (including the use of words) likely to cause disorder or a breach of the peace;

29. failure to move any chair, stand or platform in the public speaking area in accordance with the request of a Park-Keeper or Police Constable;

30. in a public speech or address the use of language (a) which is obscene, insulting, blasphemous or threatening, or (b) imparting or purporting to impart information concerning racing or betting, or indicating that such information can be obtained elsewhere, or (c) that any article, commodity, facility or service can be obtained whether in the Park or elsewhere.

III. Acts for Which Written Permission is Required

Within the Park the following acts are prohibited unless the written permission of the Minister has first been obtained:

1. driving or riding any vehicle off the roads other than a hand propelled invalid carriage or any other vehicle, not being mechanically propelled, which is driven or ridden by a child of ten years of age or under and no wheel of which (including the tyre) exceeds twenty inches in diameter[1];

2. driving or using any vehicle (a) designed to seat more than seven passengers (in addition to the driver), or (b) constructed or adapted for the purpose of any trade or business or as a dwelling, other than a vehicle designed to seat not more than seven passengers (in addition to the driver) and used only for the carriage of passengers and their effects pursuant to a contract for the use of the vehicle as a whole except in either case for the purpose of transacting business with persons residing in the Park or using land under any licence from the Minister, or for removing any vehicle which has broken down in the Park;

3. driving or riding any vehicle on any road declared closed by notice;

4. riding except on the riding ways;

5. leaving a vehicle unattended elsewhere than in a place for the time being appointed by the Minister for that purpose;

6. entering or being in the Park at any time when it is not open to public;

7. going on any enclosure, flower bed or shrubbery, or on any lawn access to which is prohibited by notice;

8. carrying on any trade or business;

9. selling or distributing anything or offering anything for sale or hire;

10. exhibiting or affixing any notice, advertisement, or other written or pictorial matter, or any display, performance, or representation;

11. making or giving a public speech or address except in the public speaking area;

12. playing or causing to be played a musical instrument;

13. organising, conducting, or taking part in any assembly, parade or procession;

14. erecting or using any apparatus for the transmission, reception, reproduction, or amplification of sound, speech or images by electrical or mechanical means, except apparatus designed and used as an aid to

---

[1] Amended by the Hyde Park (Second Amendment) Regulations, 1965

defective hearing and apparatus used in a vehicle so as not to produce sound audible by a person outside the vehicle;

15. discharging a firearm or lighting a fire or firework;
16. fishing or camping;
17. causing or permitting a boat to be on any water;
18. going on any ice when a notice is exhibited prohibiting so doing.

IV. General

1. A Park Keeper or Police Constable who is of opinion that disorder or a breach of the peace is likely to arise from any public speaking may request any person who has spoken or who appears to intend to speak publicly to move to some other place indicated to him in the public speaking area before speaking or continuing to speak publicly and that person shall comply with the request.

2. Any person who has contravened any of these Regulations shall on demand by a Park Keeper or Police Constable give his name and address.

V. Revocation of Previous Regulations

The Hyde Park Regulations, 1950[1], are hereby revoked.

VI. Commencement These Regulations shall come into operation on the expiry of fourteen days after the day on which they are made.

Dated this 22nd day of November, 1955.

Given under the Official Seal of the Minister of Works. (L.S.)

NIGEL BIRCH,
Minister of Works.

---

[1] S.I. 1950/2214.

Bibliography

by Jim Huggon

Reprinted here in part or whole:

Bonar Thompson: *Hyde Park Orator* (London: Jarrolds, 1934; Baltimore: Union of Egoists 2020). Still the best book that has the most of interest to say about Speakers' Corner. See page 65.

Donald Soper: *Tower Hill 12.30* (London: Epworth Press, 1963). Lord Soper's own story of his experiences over forty years and more open-air speaking at London's other speaker's corner. See page 91.

David Rubinstein (ed.): *People for the People* (London: Ithaca Press, 1973). See page 37.

Antonia Raeburn: *Militant Suffragettes* (London: Michael Joseph, 1973). See page 51.

David Fernbach (ed.): *Karl Marx: Surveys from Exile.* (Harmondsworth: Penguin Books, 1973). See page 27.

Eric J. Hobsbawn (ed.) *Labour's Turning Point 1880-1900* ([London:] Harvester Press 1974). See page 49.

William Kent: *An Encyclopaedia of London* (London: Dent, 1970). See page 23.

HMSO: *The Parks' Regulation Acts, 1872 and 1926, with Regulations for Hyde Park, 1955 as amended by The Hyde Park (First Amendment) Regulations, 1960, and The Hyde Park Regulations (Second Temporary Amendment) Order, 1961..* Compulsory reading for any would-be orator... or heckler. See page 117.

Socialist Party of Great Britain: "*Socialist Standard* Seventieth Anniversary Issue." Vol. 70 No 838 (June 1974). See page 103.

Dona Torr: *Tom Mann and His Times 1890-92* (London: London : History Group of the Communist Party, 1962). See page 43.

Time Out. London (3-9 May 1974). See page 114.

Guy Aldred: *No Traitor's Gait* (Glasgow: Strickland Press 1957). See page 57.

Freedom Defense Committee: *Freedom Defense Committee Bulletin* Nos. 1-7 (1946-1948). See page 89.

Also of interest:

Douglas Thompson: *Donald Soper: A Biography* (Nutfield: Denholm House Press, 1971) and William Purcell: *Portrait of Soper* (London: Mowbrays, 1972). Two works on one of the finest, and certainly the best known, of contemporary Hyde Park speakers.

Heathcote Williams: *The Speakers* (London: Hutchins, 1964). A highly praised but, in my view, overrated book on four post-war speakers, Axel Ney-Hock, Jacobus van Dyn, Webster and MacGinness.

Jack Lindsay: *William Morris* (London: Constable, 1975).

Eric J. Batson: "G. B. S.: The Orator and the Man" (*English: Journal of the English Association*, Volume 14, Issue 81, Autumn 1962, Pages 97–100).

Clive Graham-Ranger: "Speakers' Corner" (*This Month in London* October 1973). Superficial.

Midge Mackenzie: *Shoulder to Shoulder* (New York: Penguin Books 1975). On the Suffragette movement, including accounts of their Hyde Park meetings and demonstrations.

Gordon Bromley: *London Goes to War - 1939* (London: Michael Joseph, 1974).

R. J. Cruikshank: *The Moods of London* (London: Hamilton 1951) esp. Chapter 5.

Ms. Alec Tweedie: *Hyde Park: Its History and Romance* (London: E. Nash, 1908; London: Besant, 1930). A jingoistic, "Hyde Park as the center of the British Empire" book, which manages to avoid practically any reference to Speakers' Corner at all.

Eric Dancy: *Hyde Park* (London: Methuen, 1937) A more interesting and informative account than Tweedie.

John A. Lee: *Simple on a Soapbox* (Christchurch: Whitcomb and Tombs, 1975) Soapboxing in New Zealand in the early part of the Century, by a man who later rose to government office in New Zealand.

Rodney Mace: *Trafalgar Square: Emblem of Empire* (London: Lawrence and Wishart, 1976) A fascinating history of another of London's great meeting places.

Robert Barltrop: *The Monument: The Story of the Socialist Party of Great Britain* (London: Pluto Press, 1975). A finely written memoir of one of the organisations who have always made good use of Speakers' Corner.

F. W. Batchelor: *Around the Marble Arch* (London: Narod Press, 1939) An interesting albeit superficial survey of Speakers' Corner in the Thirties, concentrating on its more humorous aspects.

George Bernard Shaw: *Shaw: An Autobiography* (Stanley Weintraub, ed.) (London: Max Reinhardt, 1971) Selected from his writings.

George Bernard Shaw: *Platform and Puplit* (Stanley Weintraub, ed.) (London: Rupert Hart-Davis, 1962).

Tom Mann: *Memoirs* (London: MacGibbon & Kee, 1967) The memoirs of one of Hyde Park's greatest speakers.

The Hyde Park Socialist Quarterly (1968-1984). An effort of one of the platforms to extend its valuable activities "outside the gates."

Albert Meltzer: *The Anarchists in London 1935-1955.* (London: Cienfiegos Press: 1976) Contains interesting reminiscences of Mat Kavanagh, Frederick Lohr, Frank Hirschfield, Philip Sansom, Rita Milton, Len Harvey, Tom Turner, Bonar Thompson and other speakers from Hyde Park, as well as being a fascinating, if idiosyncratic, view of anarchists in London.

Select Works By or Published by Jim Juggon
Chronological. Kropotkin's Lighthouse Publications unless stated.

Bibliography on Peace, Freedom and Nonviolence for Use in Schools (1971)
A Report of Speeches and Discussions from the Anarchist Summer Camp Cornwall, England, 1969 (1973)
The Mask of Anarchy by Percy Bysshe Shelley (1973)
Libertarian Readings from William Blake, Percy Bysshe Shelley, D. H. Lawrence, Joe Hill, Bartolomeo Vanzetti, Gerrard Winstanley, Pierre-Joseph Proudhon: A Short Anthology (1973)
But Mr. Speaker, It Would Create Anarchy! (Pilton: Clarion, 1975)
Speakers' Corner: an Anthology (1977)

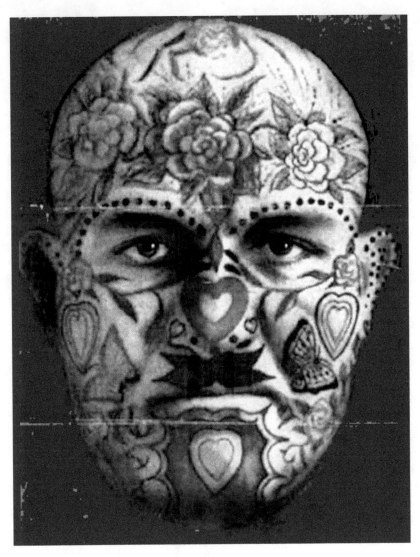

Jacobus Van Dyn

Further Reading

Hyde Park Orator Illustrated
by Bonar Thompson

The Gospel According to Malfew Seklew
by Malfew Seklew

Confessions of a Failed Egoist
by Trevor Blake

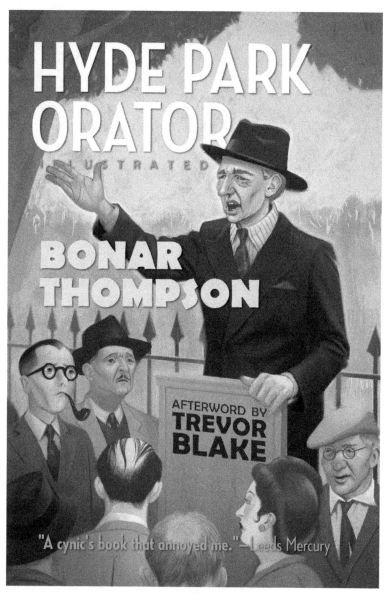

Baltimore: Underworld Amusements, 2020. ISBN 978-1-944651-18-3

Hyde Park Orator Illustrated

by Bonar Thompson

Bonar Thompson, the famous Hyde Park Orator, delighted millions of listeners at the well-known meeting-ground for many years with his dramatic personality and oratorical flights. This book, which is the story of his life, is a veritable human document. Born in Ulster to poor parents, left to struggle for himself at an early age, lacking any formal education and obliged to labor in the fields. Bonar Thompson began quite early to exhibit those unusual qualities of mind and character that have made him the social rebel he is. He describes how he taught himself to become a public speaker, threw in his lot with revolutionaries, went to prison in Manchester as an agitator, and finally lost faith in all political theories. He has some pungent things to say about his ex-comrades in the Labour and Socialist movements as well as some interesting stories about many famous men and women whom he met in the course of his very varied career. His appreciation of Shakespeare is on par with any academic.

Hyde Park Orator Illustrated by Bonar Thompson is a most unusual book and is full of entertainment from beginning to end. Newly typeset and expanded autobiography of the greatest free thinker ever to grace Speakers Corner.

With illustrations, index, bibliography, and an afterword exclusive to this edition.

"A somewhat irritating but entertaining book." - *Socialist Standard.*

The Gospel According to Malfew Seklew

by Malfew Seklew

"[Malfew Seklew] had read a great deal and had been profoundly influenced by writers like Nietzsche and Max Stirner. Their doctrines, however, had been passed through the witty and original mind of a man who possessed certain odd qualities of his own. [...] I became friendly with him and learned a great deal from one who was a distinct and outstanding personality of the market and the public square."

- Bonar Thompson, *Hyde Park Orator Illustrated.*

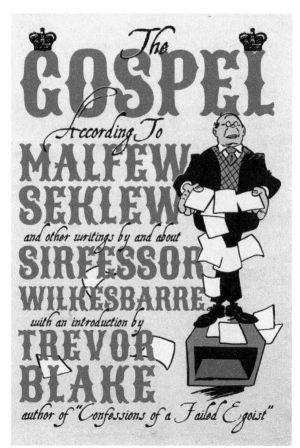

Baltimore: Underworld Amusements, 2014. ISBN 978-0988553682

Baltimore: Underworld Amusements, 2014. ISBN 978-0988553651

Confessions of a Failed Egoist

"Egoism is the claim that the individual is the measure of all things. In ethics, in epistemology, in aesthetics, in society, the Individual is the best and only arbitrator. Egoism claims social convention, laws, other people, religion, language, time and all other forces outside of the Individual are an impediment to the liberty and existence of the Individual. Such impediments may be tolerated but they have no special standing to the Individual, who may elect to ignore or subvert or destroy them as He can. In egoism the State has no monopoly to take tax or wage war."

- Trevor Blake, author of *Confessions of a Failed Egoist*, editor of *The Gospel According to Malfew Seklew* and *Hyde Park Orator Illustrated*.

"*Confessions of a Failed Egoist* is somewhere at the crossroads between *The Satanic Bible* and *Prometheus Rising*. Everything you know is wrong, but don't worry: It's just the punchline to the great epistemic joke. Blake's book is a throwback to the days of H. L. Mencken mercilessly skewering sacred cows on the left and right, while firmly rooted in our present day victimology industry conundrums. Blake's book provides inspiration for thought. Bring it up at your next boring work party and scare your colleagues."

- Nicholas Pell.

"Trevor Blake hails and assails the 'isms' closest to his heart in a Mencken-like step-right-up, soapbox style that is smart, dense and fun to read. Blake is a meticulous thinker, and this book is bound to delight and challenge individualists, egoists, and people who would dramatically object to the idea of egoism–but then do and say exactly what they want to anyway."

- Jack Donovan, author of *The Way of Men*.

"It's hard to know [who] will like this book. I'm left-wing and I really enjoyed it but I also know a bunch of people who are themselves extremely left-wing who would loathe this book because they are left-wing in a different manner than I am left-wing. If you are a liberal who is sick of victim culture, attempts at censorship on behalf of the goals of identity politics, and the denial of personal responsibility as a social good, you will like this book. Ironically, many right-wingers who are also libertarian in their mindset will hate this book because it cuts Ayn Rand little slack and refuses to pander to Christian or doctrinaire morality. So I have no idea if you will like this book. Having a deep appreciation for word play and sarcasm will help... "

- Anita Dalton, author of *Odd Things Considered*.

Index

Ballad of Reading Gaol (Wilde) 80

1867, Disraeli, Gladstone and Revolution (Cowling) 42

Agitator of the Underworld, An (Thompson) 76, 77
Agnostic Journal 60
Alderson, Lynn 13
Aldred, Guy 57
"Allan" (of the Engineers) 38
"Allen" (Christian Evidence Society) 59, 60
Allgood, Sara 67
Anderson, Alex 103
Anglia U Progu Demarkracji 42
Anti-Socialist Union 60
Applegarth, Robert 38
Around the Marble Arch (Batchelor) 25
Augusta, Lady Gregory 68
Aveling, Edward 43, 44, 46

"Bailey" (Christian Evidence Society) 60
Baker, Christian 61
"Banks" (Police inspector) 29, 32
Banner Bright (Gorman) 13
Baritz, Moses 103
Barton, N. J. 23
Batchelor, F. W. 25
Baxter, Beverley 80
Beales, Edmond 39, 40
Before the Socialists (Harrison) 37, 42
Bishop, John 9
Bismark, Otto 40
Black Hat, The (Thompson and Kelly) 14, 68, 71, 72, 77, 81
Blackwood's Magazine 61
Bligh, James 29
Boswell, James 23
Bradlaugh, Charles 46, 59
"Bray" (Christian Evidence Society) 60

"Brennan" (Police inspector) 32
Bright, John 40, 41
British Broadcasting Company 6, 65, 66
British Secular Society 60
British Socialist Party 103
"Browen" (Christian Evidence Society) 60
Brown, William 73, 81
Bulletin 37
Burns, John 43, 44, 46, 103

Caltabiano, Adolfo 89
Campaign for Nuclear Disarmament 7, 22
Campbell, Douglas 82
Capone, Al 109
Carlile, Richard 58
Carlyle, Thomas 23
Casson, Ann 81, 82
Casson, Lewis 81, 82
Central Committee for the Eight Hours Legal Working Day 43, 44
Chartists 28, 29, 31, 37–40, 46
Chesterton, G. K. 25
Christ, Jesus 86, 94, 96–99
Christian Evidence Society 57–61
Christian VII 23
Church Times 85
Churchill, Winston 74
Cloete, Stephanie 13
Clubman 104
Communist Party of Great Britain 43, 103, 104
Conservative Party 69
Conway, Moncure 57
Cooper, Ashley 27
Cowling, Maurice 42
Cromwell, Oliver 19, 23

Daily Telegraph 85
Daily Worker 85
"Darkin" (Police inspector) 32
Disraeli, Benjamin 39–41
Divine Light 110
Dockers' Union 45
Drummond, Charles 44
Drummond, Flora "The General" 52
Duke of Devonshire 23
Duke of Richmond 23
Dwyer, Bill 14

Earl of Albemarle 23
Eight Hours Movement, The (Mann) 45

INDEX

Engel, Friedrich 46
Evangel of Unrest, The (Thompson) 77
Evelyn, John 23
Evening News 85
Evening Standard 80

Fance, Edith 61
Felton, John 19
Fenbach, David 13
Finlen, James 29
Flowell, George 42
Foot, Michael 7, 37, 89
Foote, G. W. 59
Forward 85
Foster, Jo 13
Fox, George 59, 60
France, Anatole 71
Freedom Defence Committee Bulletin 89
Freedom 9, 85, 89
Freedom Defence Committee 89

Garibaldi, Giuseppe 21, 24, 40
Garland, Judy 108
George II 23
George III 23
George IV 28
"Gibbs" (Superintendent) 32
Gladstone, William 38–41
God's Protectors (Pack) 61
Gorman, John 13
Graham, Cunninghame 44, 46
"Green" (Christian Evidence Society) 60
Grosvenor, Robert 28, 31, 34
Groves, Cliff 103, 105
Guardian, The 115

Hamilton, James 23
Hardy, Thomas 54
Harris, Stanley 80
Harrison, Royden 37, 42
Henderson, Fred 45
Henry VIII 23
Hewitt ("danced on the frozen Serpentine") 24
Himmelfarb, Gertrude 42
Hirshfield, Frank 10
Hisotry of Henry Esmond, The (Thackeray) 24
Hitler, Adolph 86, 104
Hobsbawm, Eric 49
Holme, Stanford 82

Holy Maid of Kent 19
Holyoake, Austin 61
Horatio 103
Howard, Frederick 60, 61
Howard, George 24
Howell, George 43
Huggon, Jim 5, 6, 13, 15, 19, 21, 125
Hughes, Dusty 107
Hunt, Henry 24
Hutchinson, Harry 67
Huxley, Julian 96
Hyde Park Orator (Thompson) 13, 25, 65, 77, 78

Independent Labour Party 73, 103
Ireton, Henry 19
Irish Republicans 108
Irving, Henry 68

James, Joseph 82
John of France 24
Jones, Jack 103
Judd, Allan 82

Karl Marx: Surveys from Exile (Fenbach, ed.) 13
Katz, Henry 42
Kavanagh, Mat 10
Kennedy, John F. 108
Kent, William 23
King Edward the Confessor 23
Kohn, Adolph 103–105

Labour Party 6, 8, 37, 38, 61, 66, 68, 85, 86, 103
Labour's Turning Point (Hobsbawm) 49
Lady Granville 30
Lafargue, Paul 46
Langton, Basil 81, 82
Lansbury, George 103
Lestor, Charlie 103
"Let Us All Be Unhappy on Sunday" (whisky hymn) 61
Leventhal, F. M. 42
Liberal Party 8, 41, 69
Liddy, David 116
London Anarchist Group 5, 8
London Trades Council 43–46
Lord Derby 39
Lord Ebrington 34
Lord Palmerston 31
Lord Soper 101
Lost Rivers (Barton) 23
Louis XVIII 24

INDEX

MacAnna, Thomas 115
Macbeth (Shakespeare) 80
MacDonald, Desmond 14
MacDonald, Ramsay 68
MacGuinness, Billy 107–110
Maga 61
Making of the Second Reform Bill, The (Smith) 42
Malatesta Club 10
Manchester Guardian 80, 103
Mann, Tom 43–47, 74, 103
Marquess of Westminster 31
Martel, Nellie 53
Marx, Eleanor 43
Marx, Karl 13, 21, 46
May Day Committee 43
Mayer, Gustave 46
Mayne, Richard 21, 24, 31, 32
McCarthy, Lillah 54
"McInnes" (Christian Evidence Society) 59
McLean, James 23
McLean, Jeannie 13
McLean, John 103
McLean, Sharley 13
McNabb, Vincent 25
Militant Suffragettes (Raeburn) 51
Mill, John 39, 40
Milton, Ernest 68
Milton, Rita 9
Mister, Sue 13
Mohum, Charles 23
Morning Post 31
Morrison, Herbert 103
Moyse, Arthur 13
Murray, Marie 116
Murray, Noel 116

Napoleon 21, 24
National Secular Society 59, 61
Neaves, Charles 61
Ney-Hoch, Axel 10, 107, 108
Nineteenth Century 44
No Traitor's Gate (Aldred) 57

Ó Dálaigh, Cearbhall 115
O'Brien, Bronterre 38
O'Casey, Sean 67, 68, 80
O'Connor, Fergus 38
O'Neil, Maire 67
O'Rourke, J. A. 67

Ogilvie, Robert 14, 107–110
Orwell, George 85
Owen, Robert 38
Oxford University Liberal Debating Society 68, 69

Pack, Ernest 60, 61
Pankhurst, Christabel 53, 54
Paoli, Pasquale 23
Parker, S. E. 10, 100
Payne-Townshend, Charlotte (wife of Shaw) 54
Peace News 85
Peace Pledge Union 85, 105
Peeke, Jim 10
People for the People (Rubinstein) 37
Pethick-Lawrence, Emmeline 51–53
Pilgrim, John 10, 14
Pitt, William 23
Plough and the Stars, The (O'Casey) 67
Plume, George 105
Poe, Edgar Allan 68
Police Gazette 32
Political Quarterly 37
Postmen's Union 49
Powys, John Cowper 82
Public Advertiser 23
Punch 43

Queen Caroline 23
Queen Elizabeth 23
Queen Victoria 29

Radio London 10
Raeburn, Antonia 51
Reform League 21, 24, 39–42
Respectable Radical (Leventhal) 42
Rety, John 10, 13, 14, 22
Reynolds's 45, 46
Robertson, Fyfe 107
Robertson, J. M. 59
Roman Catholic Church 9
Rooum, Donald 10
Rubin, Jack 10
Rubinstein, David 37
Russell "an old man" 34
Russell, Bertrand 37
Russell, John 37, 39

Saint in Hyde Park, A (Siderman) 25
Salvation Army 93, 97, 108, 110
Sansom, Philip 5, 13, 14

INDEX

Secularist Manual of Songs and Ceremonies (Holyoake and Watts) 61
Seklew, Malfew 134
Seymour, Isabel 51
Shakespeare, William 80, 82
Shaw, Bernard 46, 54
Sheppard, John 19
Shipton, George 44, 45
Siderman, E. A. 25
Sinclair, Arthur 67
Smith, F. B. 42
Smithers, Waldron 105
Social Democratic Federation 44, 46, 103
Socialist Standard 103
Socialist International 43
Socialist Party of Great Britain 8, 103–105, 108
Songs and Verses, Social and Scientific (Neaves) 61
Soper, Donald 13, 91
Speakers, The (Williams) 10, 107, 109, 110, 115
Spectator 85
Stagg, Frank 116
Star 45, 49
Stepniak, Sergey 46
Straite, Charles 82
Synge, John 68

Tablet 85
Taylor, Robert 58
Thackeray, William 24
Thomas, Julia 13
Thompson, Bonar 12–14, 25, 65, 71
Thompson, Godfrey 23
Thorne, Will 46
Tillett, Ben 13, 35, 44, 45
Time Out 107
Times 32
Torr, Dona 43
Tory Party 39, 40
Tower Hill 12.30 (Soper) 13, 91
Trade Unionism old and New 43
Trade Unionists 43
Tribune 37, 80, 85
Truth 85
Tuke, Mabel "Pansy" 51
Turner, Peter 14
Turner, Tony 8, 103, 104

Upon Westminster Bridge (Wordsworth) 76

Van Dyn, Jacobus 107–109, 129

Victorian Minds (Himmelfarb) 42
Victorian Studies 37
Vienna Arbeiterzeitung 46
Villiers, George 19
Voltaire 28, 71

"Walker" (Superintendent) 32
Walpole, Horace 23
Walpole, Spencer 40
War Commentary (see *Freedom*) 85
Warbeck, Perkin 19
Ward, John 46
Watts, Charles 61
Webb, Beatrice 37
Webb, Sidney 37
Webster, John 107, 108
Wells, H. G. 54
Wesley, John 93
West, Benjamin 24
Whig Party 39, 42
Wilde, Oscar 80, 82
Williams, Heathcote 10, 107, 109, 115
Wilson, Nigel 14
Witcop, Rose 57
Women's Social and Political Union 51
Wootton, Barbara 104
Wordsworth, William 76
Worker, The 77

Yeats, William Butler 68
Young Communist League 104

Zangwill, Israel 54
Zapata, Emiliano 9

CPSIA information can be obtained
at www.ICGtesting.com
Printed in the USA
LVHW080446300422
717028LV00005B/118